BEST
PHOTOSHOP
FILTERS

BEST
PHOTOSHOP
FILTERS

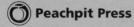 Peachpit Press

Susannah Hall

BEST PHOTOSHOP FILTERS

Peachpit Press
1249 Eighth Street
Berkeley, CA 94710
510/524-2178
510/524-2221 (fax)

Find us on the Web at: www.peachpit.com
To report errors, please send a note to errata@peachpit.com

Peachpit Press is a division of Pearson Education
Acquisitions Editor: Nikki Echler McDonald
Production Editors: Cory Borman, Hilal Sala
Proofreader: Jan Seymour

Copyright © 2012 Quarto Inc.

A QUARTO BOOK
Conceived, designed, and produced by
Quarto Publishing plc., The Old Brewery,
6 Blundell Street, London N7 9BH

Senior Editor: Katie Crous
Technical Editor: Steve Luck
Art Director: Caroline Guest
Assistant Art Editor: Kate Ormes
Assistant Designer: Alison van Kerkhoff
Picture Researcher: Sarah Bell
Proofreader: Karolin Thomas
Indexer: Diana LeCore
Quarto Creative Director: Moira Clinch
Quarto Publisher: Paul Carslake

ISBN 13 978-0-321-75422-6
ISBN 10   0-321-75422-0

10 9 8 7 6 5 4 3 2 1

Color separation by Modern Age
Printed in China by 1010 Printing International Ltd.

Contents

INTRODUCTION

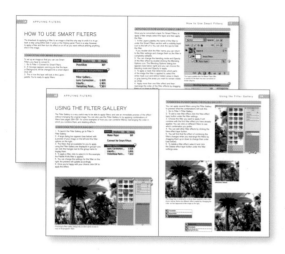

Welcome to *Best Photoshop Filters*. Whether you've used Photoshop filters before or never played around with them, this book should provide you with lots of ideas and an in-depth look into the different effects you can achieve.

You might use this book as a reference to flick through, to see which effects catch your eye, or you might choose to peruse the pages more systematically, to better understand the impact of each of the filters and its settings.

Filters offer you the opportunity to retouch and "correct" photos, as well as the facility to change

FILTER GALLERY

The filters in this section feature in the Photoshop Filter Gallery, which is toward the top of the Filter menu. For each filter in the Filter Gallery (pages 28–283) you'll find an introduction that summarizes the main uses of the filter and the options available. For information about filters not available in the Filter Gallery, see pages 10–11.

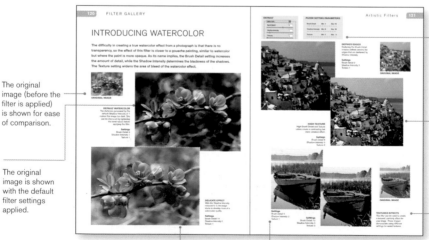

The original image (before the filter is applied) is shown for ease of comparison.

The original image is shown with the default filter settings applied.

The same image is shown with different settings applied, which produce a more pleasing or different result than the default settings.

The settings used are shown near the relevant image.

Both the default settings and the filter setting parameters are shown at the top of the page, for reference.

Further possibilities are explored with different images and settings, giving you an idea of the range of effects the featured filter can produce.

A short description of the filter's effect with the chosen settings applied is provided for each image or pair of images.

your photo so that it resembles a painting or line drawing. There are everyday filters like Unsharp Mask or Smart Sharpen—which are used on most reproduced digital photographs—and filters, such as Neon Glow, that you might use only rarely for more extreme effects.

In all the years I've been using Photoshop filters (since their creation), I've marveled at how many different effects can be achieved by altering the settings. This book lays out those effects for you to see, demonstrating the extreme effects that filters can achieve, and, equally, showing filters that produce very similar results: no need to spend time experimenting with different filters when the differences are so marginal. Peruse and enjoy!

After the introduction, the filter is explored in more detail, breaking down each setting and its effects and showcasing the full range of effects available from changing multiple settings at the same time.

The original image (before the filter is applied) is shown for ease of comparison.

The original image is shown with the default filter settings applied.

Each setting is explored in turn, with regular incremental changes applied to each image, so you can see clearly the effect of changing each setting in isolation, while the other settings remain at default.

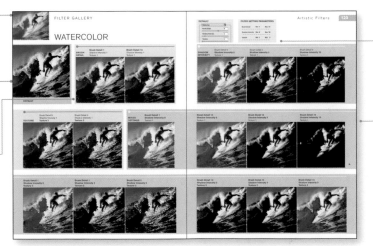

Both the default settings and the filter setting parameters are shown at the top of the page, for reference.

The Mixed Settings section contains a gallery of the most aesthetically pleasing and/or most noticeable effects that can be achieved by changing two or more of the settings from their default value.

COMBINING FILTERS

The Combining Filters section (pages 284–291) offers a taste of the visual effects that you can achieve when you apply more than one filter to an image.

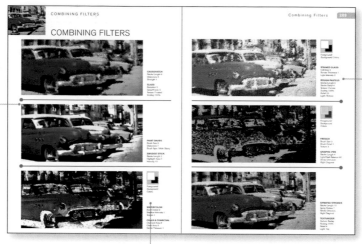

The name of the filter and the settings feature next to the relevant image.

The effects are clear to see in these large images.

Where relevant, the Foreground and Background Colors used are shown.

THE SCOPE OF FILTERS

The Scope of Filters (pages 292–325) explores the possibilities of using fade and blending modes in conjunction with filters.

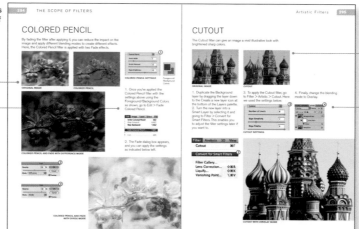

The original image (before the filter is applied) is shown for ease of comparison.

Numbered step-by-step instructions enable you to create the same effect on an image of your choice.

The original image is shown with the filter applied.

Numbered screen shots of the settings and menus correspond to the instructions.

The end result is shown, with the additional elements—fade and/or blending modes—applied to the filtered image.

OTHER FILTER EFFECTS

The Other Filter Effects section (pages 326–411) covers the filters that you can find through Photoshop's Filters menu, rather than in the Filter Gallery.

Where relevant, the default settings and the filter setting parameters are shown at the top of the page, for reference. A few filters do not have any settings at all.

The original image (before the filter is applied) is shown for ease of comparison.

Further possibilities are explored with different images and settings, giving you an idea of the range of effects the featured filter can produce.

A short description of the filter's effect with the chosen settings applied is provided for each image or couple of images.

The original image is shown with the default filter settings applied.

The same image is shown with different settings applied, which produce a more pleasing or different result than the default settings.

The settings used are shown near the relevant image.

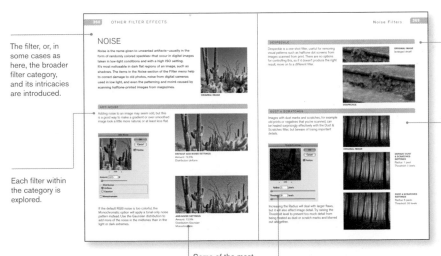

The filter, or, in some cases as here, the broader filter category, and its intricacies are introduced.

Where relevant, detail within an image is focused on, so that you can see the filter at its best effect.

As with other filters in the book, "before and after" images are shown for ease of comparison.

Each filter within the category is explored.

Some of the most useful settings are featured, showing how to solve problems by applying the filter at the correct levels.

Screen shots help you to see the relevant settings and their values.

WHAT ARE FILTERS?

Filters are applied to a photograph to manipulate the visual appearance of the final image. The filters available within Photoshop vary widely in the affect they have on an image. The biggest selection are filters that change the aesthetics of the image, making it much more artistic and unique by applying a range of effects. Other filters are designed to improve an image, such as the Lens Correction, Sharpen, and Noise filters, for example.

FILTERS USED TO CREATE ARTISTIC EFFECTS

The first place to start if you want a filter that applies an artistic effect is the Filter Gallery. When you select the Filter Gallery, a whole swathe of filters are available for you to choose from and preview through thumbnail samples. See pages 18–19 for more information about using the Filter Gallery.

ORIGINAL IMAGE

The Filter Gallery with the Accented Edges filter applied.

FILTERS USED PRIMARILY FOR RETOUCHING

There are a range of filters that can be used for different retouching purposes. Some are filters that serve little other purpose, such as the Sharpen filters. Others cross over and are useful both for retouching and for applying artistic effects, such as the Blur filters. For further information on these filters, see page 326 onward.

ORIGINAL IMAGE

After applying the Smart Sharpen filter using the default settings.

HOW TO APPLY FILTERS

There are a wide variety of Photoshop filters, and in addition to those available in the program, you can download many more. Here we explain the different ways you can apply the filters, and the difference between applying them to an image in the RGB or CMYK color mode. The filters can be applied to images, layers, or selections.

APPLYING A FILTER

It's very straightforward to apply a filter to your image.
1. Go the Filter menu and choose the filter you want to apply from the menu.
2. You might need to choose from a submenu, as with the example shown here.
The filter is then applied.

ORIGINAL IMAGE

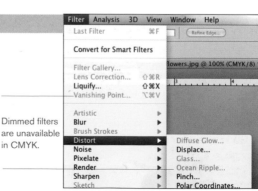

Applying the Find Edges filter. ②

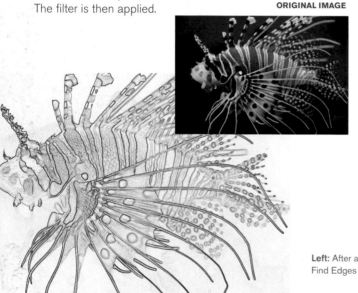

Left: After applying the Find Edges filter.

RGB AND CMYK COLOR MODES

You may be confused by the fact that if you're working with an image that is CMYK, some of the filters appear to be unavailable. They are! These are the filters (shown right) that are dimmed.

Dimmed filters are unavailable in CMYK.

The main difference between CMYK and RGB options is that the filters from the Filter Gallery, and Lens Correction and Vanishing Point, are not available for CMYK.

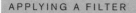

3. Alternatively, your chosen filter may take you to the settings. These take various forms to give you the control you need over the effect. Generally, sliders and percentage boxes will give you options on size of marks, tone, depth of edges, and background textures. Some filters have preview boxes to help you visualize the effect and the range of options within it. A selection of the settings you'll come across are shown here. The example to the right—one of the most complex—shows the Wave filter (Filter > Distort > Wave). The settings control a wave generator, the distance between wave peaks, the height of the waves, and the wave shape—see pages 364–365.

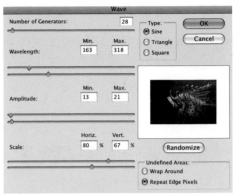

Settings for the Wave filter, as applied to the image below.

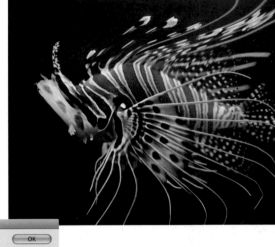

Settings for the Ripple filter.

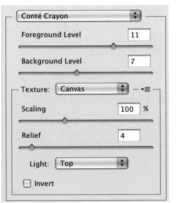

Settings for the Conté Crayon filter.

Settings for the Extrude filter.

The easiest way to deal with the lack of available filters for CMYK files is to temporarily convert your file to an RGB file, and then convert it back to a CMYK file once you have applied the filter you want.

To convert your file:

1. Go to Image > Mode > RGB. Your image will change to an RGB file.

2. Turn it back to a CMYK file by going to Image > Mode > CMYK.

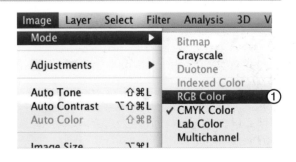

HOW TO USE SMART FILTERS

The drawback to applying a filter to an image is that the only way to undo it is to go back a step using either Edit > Undo or the History panel. There is a way, however, to apply a filter and then turn its effect on or off as you want without altering anything else in the image.

CONVERTING FOR SMART FILTERS

To set up an image so that you can use Smart Filters, you have to convert it.
1. Go to Filter > Convert for Smart Filters.
2. A message appears warning you that the layer, or Background, will be changed into a smart object. Click OK.
3. This is how the layer will look in the Layers palette. You're ready to apply filters.

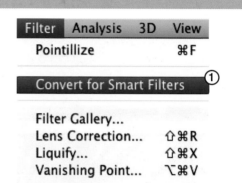

This message warns that Photoshop will create a layer that is a smart object.

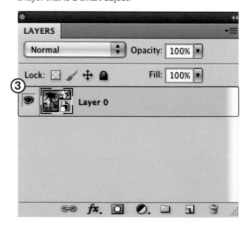

APPLYING FILTERS USING A SMART OBJECT

Once you've converted a layer for Smart Filters, to apply a filter simply select the layer and then apply the filter.

1. In the Layers palette, the name of the filter is under the Smart Filters section with a visibility (eye) icon to the left of it. You can click the eye to hide the filter.

If you double-click the filter name, you can return to the filter settings and change them so the filter is completely editable.

2. You can change the blending mode and Opacity of the filter effect by double-clicking the Blending Options icon. The Blending Options dialog box appears (see below right) and you can choose the blending mode and Opacity to apply.

3. To apply a mask that determines which parts of the image the filter is applied to, select the white mask icon and define hidden areas in black or gray, leaving the areas you want to remain visible as white.

4. Apply more than one filter effect and then rearrange the order of the filter effects by dragging them up or down in the list.

5. If you want to delete the filter effect altogether, click and drag the filter down to the Trash in the bottom right corner of the Layers palette.

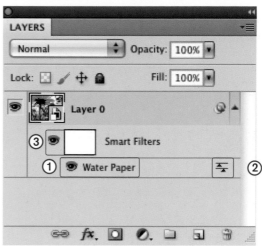

The Layers palette after the Water Paper filter is applied to the layer that was converted for Smart Objects.

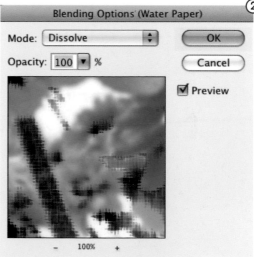

The Blending Options dialog box.

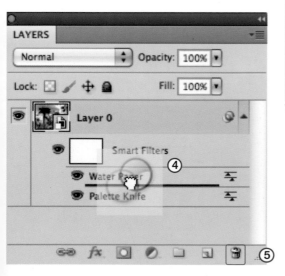

USING THE FILTER GALLERY

The Filter Gallery is a very useful way to be able to apply filters and see an immediate preview of the effect without changing the original image. You can also use the Filter Gallery to try applying combinations of filters (see pages 284–291 for some examples of how you can combine filters), rearranging the order in which you combine them, and deleting effects.

LAUNCHING THE FILTER GALLERY

1. To launch the Filter Gallery, go to Filter > Filter Gallery.
2. A large dialog box appears (see below) with a preview of your image on the left and the filter options on the right.
3. The filters that are available for you to apply using the Filter Gallery are displayed in groups—you can click the triangle next to the group name to display them.
4. To apply a filter, click to select it. In this example, the Palette Knife filter is applied.
5. You can change the settings for the filter on the right; the preview will update accordingly.
6. Once you're happy with your choice, click OK to apply the effect.

Filter	Analysis	3D	View
Water Paper			⌘F

Convert for Smart Filters

Filter Gallery...   ①
Lens Correction...   ⇧⌘R
Liquify...   ⇧⌘X
Vanishing Point...   ⌥⌘V

Photoshop's Filter Gallery dialog box provides quick access to many of the program's filters.

COMBINING FILTERS USING THE FILTER GALLERY

You can apply several filters using the Filter Gallery to preview what the combinations will look like.

1. Go to Filter > Filter Gallery.
2. To add a new filter effect, click the New effect layer button under the filter settings.
3. Choose the filter you want to apply. It will combine with the first filter effect you have already applied. You can click on different filters to see which combination you prefer.
4. You can add other filter effects by clicking the New effect layer button.
5. You will find that the effect of combining the filters changes when you rearrange the filters by dragging them up or down to change their order (see below).
6. To delete a filter effect, select it and click the Delete effect layer button under the filter settings area.

ORIGINAL IMAGE

This image has a combination of three filters applied in the order shown below. Notice the different effect created by changing the order, as has happened in the image to the right.

👁	Crosshatch
👁	Palette Knife
👁	Sprayed Strokes

👁	Palette Knife
👁	Crosshatch
👁	Sprayed Strokes

FADING A FILTER EFFECT

Once you've applied a filter effect, Photoshop offers the option to fade it. The Fade command allows you to change the opacity of the filter effect and apply a variety of blending modes. Reducing the opacity minimizes the effect of the filter, and changing the blending mode can create many different and interesting effects. See "The Scope of Filters" on pages 292–325 for some examples.

FADING A FILTER EFFECT

1. The Fade command is available only after you've applied a filter, so the first step is to apply a filter to your image.
2. Go to Edit > Fade "name of filter you have applied." In this instance, the Charcoal filter is used.
3. In the dialog box, you can change the Opacity and the (blending) Mode.

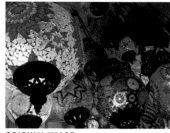

ORIGINAL IMAGE

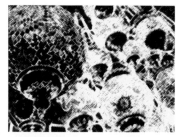

Showing the effect of the Fade command: the Opacity has been reduced slightly and the blending mode changed to Exclusion. This creates interesting color shifts, with many of the orange hues changing to blue hues.

After the Charcoal filter is applied.

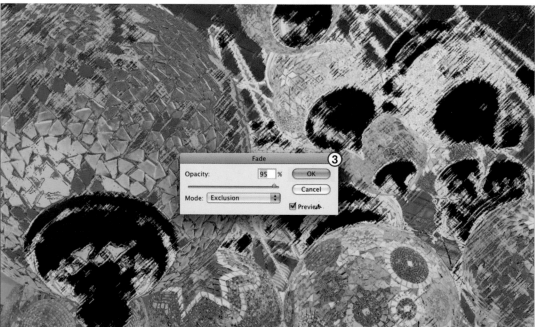

USING DUPLICATE LAYERS

Duplicating the image layer before you apply the filter allows you to adjust the filter at a later stage. Although it may seem simpler to convert the layer into a Smart Object so that you can edit the filter afterward, there are times when you may want to apply different filters and masks for each filter effect, in which case it is necessary to duplicate the layer.

USING DUPLICATE LAYERS

1. To duplicate your image layer, drag it down to the Create a new layer icon at the bottom of the Layers palette. The duplicate layer will appear with "copy" added to the name.

2. In this example, the top layer has the Dry Brush filter applied, along with a mask that leaves the horse untouched. The middle layer has the Poster Edges filter applied, but due to the mask on the top layer it appears to apply only to the horse.

3. You can then use different Opacity levels and blending modes to adjust the image further.

ORIGINAL IMAGE

The final image: The top layer has the Dry Brush filter applied, and the middle layer has the Poster Edges filter applied.

USING THE HISTORY BRUSH

It's often useful to use the History Brush to apply a filter effect to specific areas of your image. You can use this technique if you want to retouch a particular part or simply to apply some localized special effects.

USING THE HISTORY BRUSH

Before you can use the History Brush, you first have to apply a filter effect and then create a snapshot. In this example, the Poster Edges filter is applied.
1. To create a snapshot, click the Create new snapshot icon at the bottom of the History palette.
2. The new snapshot appears at the top of the History palette. It's good practice to give it a name, so you can remember what it represents.
3. Select the History Brush Tool in the toolbox.

To paint in the filter effect with the History Brush, click the box beside the snapshot to set the source for the History Brush. You also need to go back a step to Open so that you're working on the image before the filter was applied.
4. In the History Brush Toolbar that appears at the top of the screen when you select the History Brush, you can choose your Brush type, blending mode, and Opacity. In this example, a Hard Round brush is used with Normal blending mode and 100% Opacity.
5. Now you're ready to paint in the filter effect over the parts of the image to which you wish to apply it.

In this image, the filter was painted in over the left half of the flower using the History Brush.

USING DIFFERENT BRUSHES WITH THE HISTORY BRUSH

You can create some very interesting effects using the History Brush in conjunction with other brushes available in Photoshop and a different blending mode.

1. In this example, the Reticulation Filter is applied, a snapshot created (see right), and the History Brush selected.

2. From the default brushes, select the Round Blunt Medium Stiff brush.

3. Go to Window > Brush to bring up the brush settings. In the Bristle Qualities section, change the settings for the brush to add more Bristles (100%) and Stiffness (100%).

4. Select the Vivid Light blending mode, and then draw lines horizontally across the image using the brush.

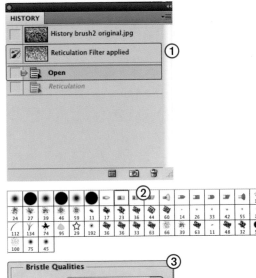

ORIGINAL IMAGE

THE FINAL IMAGE

FINDING NEW FILTERS

There are a myriad different web sites, of individual developers and larger organizations, that offer Photoshop filters to download. The cost of the filters range from free to several hundred dollars. Here are some sites to have a look at:

FINDING NEW FILTERS

There are some additional filters for Photoshop that you can download from Adobe. Go to http://labs.adobe.com/technologies/pixelbenderplugin and follow the instructions. You could also try Adobe's Pixel Bender Exchange for some other free filters.

Although most sources will require you to pay, the best place to start looking for new plug-ins is probably the Adobe Photoshop Marketplace. Go to www.adobe.com/go/psmarketplace.

These are some companies you could investigate that have useful and reliable filters to download:
* www.digitalanarchy.com
* www.alienskin.com
* www.pixelan.com
* www.prodigitalsoftware.com
* www.mehdiplugins.com/index.htm
* www.alphaplugins.com/index.php

Also try Texture Anarchy—www.digitalanarchy.com/texture/main.html—a set of three Photoshop filters that give you some useful textures and borders.

text & selection filters:

Backlight · Bevel · Chrome · Corona · Drip · Extrude · Fire · Glass · Gradient Glow

texture filters:

Animal Fur · Brick Wall · Brushed Metal · Diamond Plate · Marble · Reptile Skin · Ripples · Squint · Stone Wall

Icicles · Motion Trail · Perspective Shadow · Rust · Smoke · Snow Drift · Super Star · Swirl · Texture Noise · Water Drops · Weave · Wood

Alien Skin offers Eye Candy—www.alienskin.com/eyecandy—which contains a large range of handy filters.

ADDING NEW FILTERS

Once you have found some additional third-party filters to add to Photoshop's own, you need to move them into the correct folder—here's how.

ADDING NEW FILTERS

Many new filters or plug-ins that you download will come with an installer that automatically loads the software into the right place. However, if you have to manually install the software, this is how you load new filters. Remember that once you have installed the filters, you will need to restart Photoshop.

On a Mac:
1. Make sure Photoshop isn't running (so Quit if it is!), open a new window, and navigate to Applications > Adobe Photoshop CS5 > Plug-ins > Filters.
2. Drag the filter into that folder and launch Photoshop. You should find that the new filter has been added to the Filters menu.

On a PC:
1. Make sure Photoshop isn't running. Navigate to the folder C:/Program Files/Adobe/Photoshop CS5/Plug-ins/Filters.
2. Drag your new filter into that folder and when you launch Photoshop you should see the new filter under the Filters menu.

In both Mac and PC versions of Photoshop, you place new filters in the Filters folder, which is in the Plug-ins folder inside the main Applications folder.

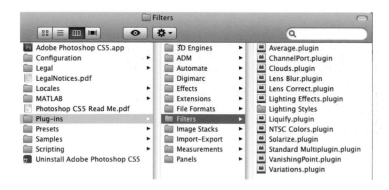

FILTER

DIRECTORY

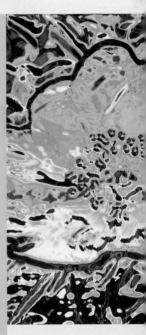

The Filter Directory is arranged over four sections: the first three sections feature filters from the Filter Gallery; the last section takes a look at the rest of the Photoshop filters.

FILTER GALLERY (PAGES 28–283)

This section covers each of the filters accessed from the Filter Gallery. Each filter is accompanied by an introduction that explains the effect of the relevant settings, followed by examples of the settings applied to an image, demonstrating the range of effects that can be achieved.

COMBINING FILTERS (PAGES 284–291)

These pages give you a taste of the vast range of possibilities available from combining filters, which you can do in the Filter Gallery.

THE SCOPE OF FILTERS (PAGES 292–325)

This section takes the filters in the Filter Gallery and demonstrates how they can be applied to create different effects using layers and the Fade Filter command.

OTHER FILTER EFFECTS (PAGES 326–411)

An overview of the rest of the Photoshop filters, which are available on the Filter menu rather than in the Filter Gallery.

FILTER GALLERY

In this part of the Filter Directory, you'll find a huge selection of different filter effects that you can use as a reference tool. The filters featured are taken from the Photoshop Filter Gallery, which is a very useful feature for being able to preview, select, and test out the filters you want to apply to your image. The gallery is almost at the top of the Filters menu in Photoshop (for an explanation of how to use the Filter Gallery, see pages 18–19).

This part of the book takes each filter* and begins with an introduction to the filter, explaining and demonstrating how it works and the effects it can produce. Each filter is then applied to the same image with a variety of different settings, so that you can see more clearly the incremental changes available under one setting and can also browse to find an effect you particularly like.

*You can't access all of Photoshop's filters through the Filter Gallery, so as with Photoshop's menus, you'll find the other filters from the specific filter menu categories covered in the Other Filter Effects section toward the back of the book. For instance, the Diffuse Glow, Glass, and Ocean Ripple filters from the Distort menu are available in the Filter Gallery (see pages 158–171), while the rest of the Distort filters (Displace, Pinch, Polar Coordinates, Ripple, Shear, Spherize, Twirl, Wave, and ZigZag) are covered in the Other Filter Effects section (see pages 350–367).

ARTISTIC FILTERS

There are 15 Artistic filters, all available through the Filter Gallery, and, as is implied by the way they're grouped, they're designed to mimic artistic effects. You can certainly produce great results with every one of the filters. Whatever the impact you're looking to make, you should find a suitable effect to work with among the myriad filters shown here.

INTRODUCING COLORED PENCIL

The Colored Pencil filter looks for defined edges to turn into pencil strokes by using the colors in an image. Larger areas of solid color are treated as plain paper, so they are replaced with a tint of the Background Color, the tint being determined by the Paper Brightness setting.

ORIGINAL IMAGE

DEFAULT COLORED PENCIL
The Colored Pencil filter turns a photograph into a sketch, giving all the detail a drawn look. Using a white Background Color with the default setting of Paper Brightness at 25 creates a gray tint "paper" color.

Foreground/
Background
Colors

Settings
Pencil Width 4
Stroke Pressure 8
Paper Brightness 25

Foreground/
Background
Colors

**BLUE/GRAY
PAPER COLOR**
Here the Background Color has been changed to a blue/gray, and you can see that the more solid areas have been replaced with that color, as though they were the paper.

Settings
Pencil Width 1
Stroke Pressure 15
Paper Brightness 25

DEFAULT

Colored Pencil	
Pencil Width	4
Stroke Pressure	8
Paper Brightness	25

FILTER SETTING PARAMETERS

Pencil Width	Min **1**	Max **24**
Stroke Pressure	Min **0**	Max **15**
Paper Brightness	Min **0**	Max **50**

ORIGINAL IMAGE

Settings
Pencil Width 5
Stroke Pressure 10
Paper Brightness 0

BLACK AND WHITE PAPER
Above: With Paper Brightness at 0, the paper turns black (regardless of the Background Color).
Right: The paper becomes white when the Paper Brightness is at its maximum value of 50, brightening the image.

Settings
Pencil Width 15
Stroke Pressure 15
Paper Brightness 50

VARYING PENCIL WIDTH
Left: With Pencil Width set very low, the lines are thin and detailed.
Below: Pencil Width is at its thickest and the outlines are much thicker, with more solid areas of background paper.

Foreground/
Background Colors

ORIGINAL IMAGE

Settings
Pencil Width 2
Stroke Pressure 15
Paper Brightness 15

Settings
Pencil Width 24
Stroke Pressure 15
Paper Brightness 15

COLORED PENCIL

Foreground/
Background
Colors

DEFAULT

PENCIL WIDTH

Pencil Width 1
Stroke Pressure 8
Paper Brightness 25

Pencil Width 12
Stroke Pressure 8
Paper Brightness 25

Pencil Width 4
Stroke Pressure 4
Paper Brightness 25

Pencil Width 4
Stroke Pressure 15
Paper Brightness 25

PAPER BRIGHTNESS

Pencil Width 4
Stroke Pressure 8
Paper Brightness 0

MIXED SETTINGS

Pencil Width 10
Stroke Pressure 2
Paper Brightness 25

Pencil Width 10
Stroke Pressure 15
Paper Brightness 25

Pencil Width 20
Stroke Pressure 2
Paper Brightness 25

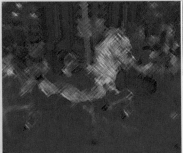

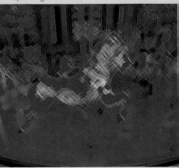

DEFAULT

Colored Pencil	▼
Pencil Width	4
Stroke Pressure	8
Paper Brightness	25

FILTER SETTING PARAMETERS

Pencil Width	Min **1**	Max **24**
Stroke Pressure	Min **0**	Max **15**
Paper Brightness	Min **0**	Max **50**

Pencil Width 20
Stroke Pressure 8
Paper Brightness 25

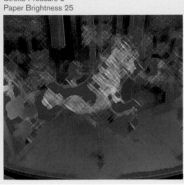

Pencil Width 24
Stroke Pressure 8
Paper Brightness 25

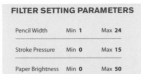

STROKE PRESSURE
Pencil Width 4
Stroke Pressure 1
Paper Brightness 25

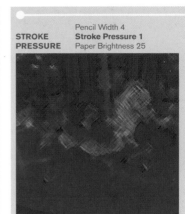

Pencil Width 4
Stroke Pressure 8
Paper Brightness 15

Pencil Width 4
Stroke Pressure 8
Paper Brightness 35

Pencil Width 4
Stroke Pressure 8
Paper Brightness 50

Pencil Width 2
Stroke Pressure 5
Paper Brightness 4

Pencil Width 24
Stroke Pressure 15
Paper Brightness 8

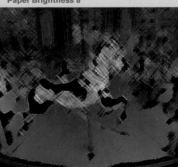

Pencil Width 24
Stroke Pressure 15
Paper Brightness 40

INTRODUCING CUTOUT

The Cutout filter turns a photograph into an image that appears to be made from cutout pieces of colored paper. It works by reducing the number of colors in the image, creating a block effect that can appear to be abstract or simplifying an image to create an Andy Warhol effect.

ORIGINAL IMAGE

DEFAULT CUTOUT
With the initial default settings applied, it is difficult to imagine it consists of pieces of cutout paper. The overall effect is more of posterization.

Settings
Levels 4
Edge Simplicity 4
Edge Fidelity 2

ABSTRACT
As the Edge Simplicity is increased, the shapes merge with jagged edges. Reducing the Edge Fidelity to 1 would create an even more abstract effect.

Settings
Levels 7
Edge Simplicity 9
Edge Fidelity 2

DEFAULT

Cutout	⬍
Number of Levels	4
Edge Simplicity	4
Edge Fidelity	2

FILTER SETTING PARAMETERS

Number of Levels	Min **2**	Max	**8**
Edge Simplicity	Min **0**	Max	**10**
Edge Fidelity	Min **1**	Max	**3**

ADJUSTING LEVELS

Left: The number of Levels has been increased to 8, which, with Edge Simplicity and Fidelity both at their extremes, gives you the most detail.

Below: Reducing the Levels to 3 decreases the number of colors, creating a less detailed version. You can experiment by reselecting the same Levels setting—the colors will change each time.

Settings
Levels 8
Edge Simplicity 0
Edge Fidelity 3

Settings
Levels 3
Edge Simplicity 0
Edge Fidelity 3

ORIGINAL IMAGE

Settings
Levels 8
Edge Simplicity 5
Edge Fidelity 3

ORIGINAL IMAGE

MOSAIC

Far left: An image with simple detail is well suited to this filter. It looks almost like a painterly effect.

Left: These settings have achieved a colored-paper mosaic look.

Settings
Levels 5
Edge Simplicity 5
Edge Fidelity 2

CUTOUT

DEFAULT

NUMBER OF LEVELS

Number of Levels 2
Edge Simplicity 4
Edge Fidelity 2

Number of Levels 3
Edge Simplicity 4
Edge Fidelity 2

Number of Levels 4
Edge Simplicity 2
Edge Fidelity 2

Number of Levels 4
Edge Simplicity 7
Edge Fidelity 2

Number of Levels 4
Edge Simplicity 10
Edge Fidelity 2

Number of Levels 7
Edge Simplicity 0
Edge Fidelity 2

Number of Levels 3
Edge Simplicity 5
Edge Fidelity 2

Number of Levels 5
Edge Simplicity 5
Edge Fidelity 1

DEFAULT

Cutout

Number of Levels	4
Edge Simplicity	4
Edge Fidelity	2

FILTER SETTING PARAMETERS

Number of Levels	Min 2	Max 8
Edge Simplicity	Min 0	Max 10
Edge Fidelity	Min 1	Max 3

Number of Levels 6
Edge Simplicity 4
Edge Fidelity 2

Number of Levels 8
Edge Simplicity 4
Edge Fidelity 2

EDGE SIMPLICITY
Number of Levels 4
Edge Simplicity 0
Edge Fidelity 2

EDGE FIDELITY
Number of Levels 4
Edge Simplicity 4
Edge Fidelity 1

Number of Levels 4
Edge Simplicity 4
Edge Fidelity 3

MIXED SETTINGS
Number of Levels 3
Edge Simplicity 0
Edge Fidelity 2

Number of Levels 5
Edge Simplicity 7
Edge Fidelity 3

Number of Levels 8
Edge Simplicity 10
Edge Fidelity 3

Number of Levels 2
Edge Simplicity 0
Edge Fidelity 1

INTRODUCING DRY BRUSH

You can achieve a variety of effects using the Dry Brush filter, creating a look that approximates something between an oil and watercolor painting. The filter reduces the number of distinct color areas (Brush Size) with the option to increase the amount of Brush Detail and change how contrasted the edges are (Texture).

ORIGINAL IMAGE

DEFAULT DRY BRUSH
You can see how the number of colors has been reduced compared to the original image (above).

Settings
Brush Size 2
Brush Detail 8
Texture 1

WATERCOLOR EFFECT
Increasing the Brush Size while keeping the Texture at its lowest creates something closer to a watercolor effect.

Settings
Brush Size 10
Brush Detail 8
Texture 1

DEFAULT

Dry Brush		
Brush Size		2
Brush Detail		8
Texture		1

FILTER SETTING PARAMETERS

Brush Size	Min 0	Max 10
Brush Detail	Min 0	Max 10
Texture	Min 1	Max 3

ORIGINAL IMAGE

Settings
Brush Size 10
Brush Detail 0
Texture 1

SOFT VS. DEFINED
Far left: With the Brush Size set to 10 and the Texture value reduced to 1, the edges become soft and blurred.
Left: Leaving the Brush Size at 10 and increasing the Texture value to 3 creates sharply defined edges.

Settings
Brush Size 10
Brush Detail 0
Texture 3

BRUSH DETAIL
Left: With the Brush Size and Brush Detail reduced, the high Texture setting creates sharply defined edges, looking almost like pen and ink on top of a painting.
Below: The Brush Detail has been increased, giving a more subtle painterly effect.

ORIGINAL IMAGE

Settings
Brush Size 0
Brush Detail 0
Texture 3

Settings
Brush Size 0
Brush Detail 10
Texture 3

DRY BRUSH

DEFAULT

BRUSH SIZE

Brush Size 10
Brush Detail 8
Texture 1

BRUSH DETAIL

Brush Size 2
Brush Detail 0
Texture 1

MIXED SETTINGS

Brush Size 0
Brush Detail 0
Texture 1

Brush Size 10
Brush Detail 0
Texture 1

Brush Size 0
Brush Detail 10
Texture 1

DEFAULT

Dry Brush	
Brush Size	2
Brush Detail	8
Texture	1

FILTER SETTING PARAMETERS

Brush Size	Min **0**	Max **10**
Brush Detail	Min **0**	Max **10**
Texture	Min **1**	Max **3**

Brush Size 2
Brush Detail 4
Texture 1

Brush Size 2
Brush Detail 8
TEXTURE **Texture 2**

Brush Size 2
Brush Detail 8
Texture 3

Brush Size 0
Brush Detail 0
Texture 3

Brush Size 10
Brush Detail 0
Texture 3

Brush Size 0
Brush Detail 10
Texture 3

INTRODUCING FILM GRAIN

The Film Grain filter is so named to imply it can replicate the slightly grainy look of a transparency or traditional photographic print. In reality the grain is too large to do that. Instead, you can use it to add some texture and to boost the highlights in an image as well as to create a range of other effects.

ORIGINAL IMAGE

DEFAULT FILM GRAIN
The Film Grain filter clumps pixels together, creating an almost posterized effect with added texture from the small dots of grain.

Settings
Grain 4
Highlight Area 0
Intensity 10

ADDING DEPTH AND TEXTURE
The filter can be used to add depth and texture by increasing the Grain and Highlight Area values.

Settings
Grain 10
Highlight Area 10
Intensity 10

DEFAULT

Film Grain	
Grain	4
Highlight Area	0
Intensity	10

FILTER SETTING PARAMETERS

Grain	Min **0**	Max **20**
Highlight Area	Min **0**	Max **20**
Intensity	Min **0**	Max **10**

VIVID COLORS

Left: Increasing the Highlight Area to its maximum creates very vivid, almost fluorescent colors in this image.

Below: The amount of grain has been increased in this image, giving more texture and slightly diminished intensity.

ORIGINAL IMAGE

Settings
Grain 4
Highlight Area 20
Intensity 10

Settings
Grain 15
Highlight Area 20
Intensity 6

Settings
Grain 0
Highlight Area 0
Intensity 2

ORIGINAL IMAGE

NO GRAIN

Reducing the Grain to 0 means you are employing the effect of the Highlight Area and Intensity without adding any texture.

Far left: This is a minimal adjustment that boosts the stone wall.

Left: Increasing the Highlight Area and Intensity creates burned-out highlights.

Settings
Grain 0
Highlight Area 16
Intensity 10

FILM GRAIN

DEFAULT

GRAIN

Grain 0
Highlight Area 0
Intensity 10

Grain 10
Highlight Area 0
Intensity 10

Grain 4
Highlight Area 10
Intensity 10

Grain 4
Highlight Area 15
Intensity 10

Grain 4
Highlight Area 20
Intensity 10

Grain 15
Highlight Area 5
Intensity 10

Grain 20
Highlight Area 10
Intensity 10

Grain 20
Highlight Area 20
Intensity 10

DEFAULT

Film Grain

Grain 4
Highlight Area 0
Intensity 10

FILTER SETTING PARAMETERS

Grain	Min	**0**	Max	**20**
Highlight Area	Min	**0**	Max	**20**
Intensity	Min	**0**	Max	**10**

Grain 15
Highlight Area 0
Intensity 10

Grain 20
Highlight Area 0
Intensity 10

HIGHLIGHT AREA

Grain 4
Highlight Area 4
Intensity 10

INTENSITY

Grain 4
Highlight Area 0
Intensity 0

Grain 4
Highlight Area 0
Intensity 5

MIXED SETTINGS

Grain 10
Highlight Area 5
Intensity 10

Grain 20
Highlight Area 20
Intensity 5

Grain 20
Highlight Area 20
Intensity 0

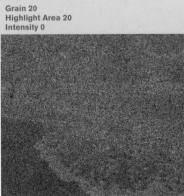

Grain 10
Highlight Area 0
Intensity 0

INTRODUCING FRESCO

You'll notice that images become darker when you apply the Fresco filter. This is because the filter adds a black overlay to the darker areas. The effects mostly bear little relationship to real-life mural paintings, although many of them are just as interesting.

ORIGINAL IMAGE

DEFAULT FRESCO
Notice how thick lines of black appear within the image, creating a contrasting effect. Much of the detail has been blurred to look painterly.

Settings
Brush Size 2
Brush Detail 8
Texture 1

ADDING TEXTURE
By decreasing the Brush Size and Brush Detail values and increasing the Texture, the black lines become much thinner, giving an overall textured effect.

Settings
Brush Size 0
Brush Detail 0
Texture 3

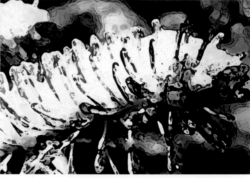

DEFAULT

Fresco	
Brush Size	2
Brush Detail	8
Texture	1

FILTER SETTING PARAMETERS

Brush Size	Min **0**	Max **10**
Brush Detail	Min **0**	Max **10**
Texture	Min **1**	Max **3**

ORIGINAL IMAGE

Settings
Brush Size 0
Brush Detail 10
Texture 3

HIGH CONTRAST

Right: Here the Brush Detail has been increased to its maximum so that the texture is less spidery and contrasts more.
Far right: The larger Brush Size means that much of the detail of the needles has become generalized, but the high Texture has generated some interesting patterns.

Settings
Brush Size 10
Brush Detail 0
Texture 3

ORIGINAL IMAGE

WATERCOLOR EFFECT

For these applications of the filter, the Texture has been reduced to 1 and the effect is much more painterly.
Far right: The low value for Brush Size means there is more detail around the edges.
Right: A watercolor effect is created from a broad Brush Size and low Texture.

Settings
Brush Size 10
Brush Detail 0
Texture 1

Settings
Brush Size 0
Brush Detail 0
Texture 1

FRESCO

DEFAULT

BRUSH SIZE

Brush Size 0
Brush Detail 8
Texture 1

Brush Size 10
Brush Detail 8
Texture 1

Brush Size 10
Brush Detail 7
Texture 1

Brush Size 0
Brush Detail 0
Texture 1

Brush Size 0
Brush Detail 0
Texture 2

DEFAULT

Fresco	
Brush Size	2
Brush Detail	8
Texture	1

FILTER SETTING PARAMETERS

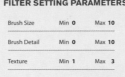

Brush Size	Min 0	Max 10
Brush Detail	Min 0	Max 10
Texture	Min 1	Max 3

BRUSH DETAIL
Brush Size 2
Brush Detail 0
Texture 1

TEXTURE
Brush Size 2
Brush Detail 8
Texture 3

MIXED SETTINGS
Brush Size 7
Brush Detail 0
Texture 1

Brush Size 0
Brush Detail 0
Texture 3

Brush Size 0
Brush Detail 10
Texture 3

Brush Size 10
Brush Detail 0
Texture 3

INTRODUCING NEON GLOW

The Neon Glow filter both colorizes an image—which means it applies a color wash over the entire image—using the Foreground Color, and then it applies a glow according to the filter settings to either the highlights (if the Glow Size is a positive value) or the shadows (if the Glow Size is a negative value).

ORIGINAL IMAGE

Foreground/
Background
Colors

**DEFAULT
NEON GLOW**
With the default blue
Glow Color and
black Foreground
Color, a black
and blue image
is the result.

Settings
Glow Size 5
Glow Brightness 15

Foreground/
Background
Colors

**CHANGING THE
FOREGROUND COLOR**
The Foreground Color
was light yellow when the
filter was applied, with
the default Glow Color
selected. With a Glow Size
of -1, the glow applies to
the shadows rather than
the highlights.

Settings
Glow Size -1
Glow Brightness 43

DEFAULT

Glow Size		5
Glow Brightness		15
Glow Color		

FILTER SETTING PARAMETERS

Glow Size	Min **-24**	Max **24**
Glow Brightness	Min **0**	Max **50**

ORIGINAL IMAGE

Foreground/
Background Colors

GRAYSCALE EFFECT

By using a black Foreground Color, the image effectively becomes grayscale, and here the glow creates an interesting effect on the waterfall.

Settings
Glow Size 24
Glow Brightness 20

NEGATIVE EFFECT

Using the same settings as above but with a negative value for the Glow Size results in a negative effect.

Settings
Glow Size -24
Glow Brightness 50

COLORED GLOWS

Using different colors for the Foreground Color and Glow Color, the glow creates soft highlights mixed with sharp, colored edges.

ORIGINAL IMAGE

Foreground/
Background
Colors

Foreground/
Background
Colors

Glow Color

Settings
Glow Size 16
Glow Brightness 30

Glow Color

Settings
Glow Size 0
Glow Brightness 35

NEON GLOW

Foreground/
Background
Colors

DEFAULT

GLOW SIZE

Glow Size -24
Glow Brightness 15

Glow Size -5
Glow Brightness 15

Glow Size 5
Glow Brightness 50

**MIXED
SETTINGS**

**Glow Size -24
Glow Brightness 5**

**Glow Size 0
Glow Brightness 25**

DEFAULT

Neon Glow

Glow Size	5
Glow Brightness	15
Glow Color	■

FILTER SETTING PARAMETERS

Glow Size	Min **-24**	Max **24**
Glow Brightness	Min **0**	Max **50**

Glow Size 24
Glow Brightness 15

GLOW BRIGHTNESS　Glow Size 5 **Glow Brightness 5**　Glow Size 5 **Glow Brightness 25**

Glow Size -24
Glow Brightness 50

Glow Size -24
Glow Brightness 25

Glow Size 24
Glow Brightness 25

INTRODUCING PAINT DAUBS

Paint Daubs does as its title implies—adds daubs of paint to create a variety of painterly effects. The filter offers a number of different brushes that can be applied. Some more closely mimic paint techniques and others create interesting creative effects that don't resemble any kind of painting.

ORIGINAL IMAGE

DEFAULT PAINT DAUBS
The default settings recreate an Impressionist painting, given the right subject.

Settings
Brush Size 8
Sharpness 7
Brush Type: Simple

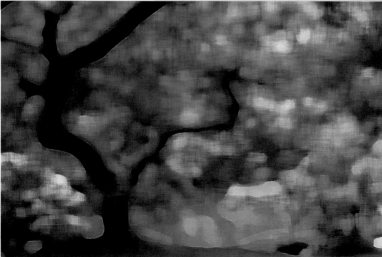

BLURRED SHARPNESS
Still using the Simple brush, this more abstract effect is achieved using a large Brush Size and high Sharpness value.

Settings
Brush Size 30
Sharpness 30
Brush Type: Simple

DEFAULT

Paint Daubs	
Brush Size	8
Sharpness	7
Brush Type:	Simple

FILTER SETTING PARAMETERS

Brush Size	Min **1**	Max **50**
Sharpness	Min **0**	Max **40**

LITHOGRAPH EFFECT
Applying both a small Brush Size and high Sharpness creates an effect that is reminiscent of a lithograph.

Settings
Brush Size 2
Sharpness 40
Brush Type: Simple

ORIGINAL IMAGE

OIL PAINTING EFFECT
You can approximate an oil painting using the Wide Blurry brush and the settings below.

Settings
Brush Size 13
Sharpness 22
Brush Type: Wide Blurry

DIFFERENT BRUSHES
Many of the other brushes create quite wild effects with distorted color glows. Here are two of the more subtle effects.

ORIGINAL IMAGE

Settings
Brush Size 5
Sharpness 4
Brush Type: Sparkle

Settings
Brush Size 32
Sharpness 7
Brush Type: Dark Rough

PAINT DAUBS
SIMPLE/LIGHT ROUGH

DEFAULT

BRUSH SIZE

Brush Size 20
Sharpness 7
Brush Type: Simple

Brush Size 50
Sharpness 7
Brush Type: Simple

DEFAULT–BRUSH TYPE: LIGHT ROUGH

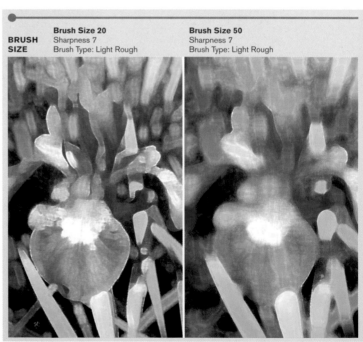

BRUSH SIZE

Brush Size 20
Sharpness 7
Brush Type: Light Rough

Brush Size 50
Sharpness 7
Brush Type: Light Rough

DEFAULT

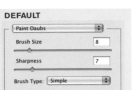

Paint Daubs

Brush Size   8

Sharpness   7

Brush Type: Simple

FILTER SETTING PARAMETERS

Brush Size	Min **1**	Max **50**
Sharpness	Min **0**	Max **40**

SHARPNESS

Brush Size 8
Sharpness 40
Brush Type: Simple

MIXED SETTINGS

Brush Size 25
Sharpness 20
Brush Type: Simple

Brush Size 50
Sharpness 40
Brush Type: Simple

SHARPNESS

Brush Size 8
Sharpness 40
Brush Type: Light Rough

MIXED SETTINGS

Brush Size 25
Sharpness 20
Brush Type: Light Rough

Brush Size 50
Sharpness 40
Brush Type: Light Rough

PAINT DAUBS
DARK ROUGH/WIDE SHARP

DEFAULT–BRUSH TYPE: DARK ROUGH

BRUSH SIZE

Brush Size 20
Sharpness 7
Brush Type: Dark Rough

Brush Size 50
Sharpness 7
Brush Type: Dark Rough

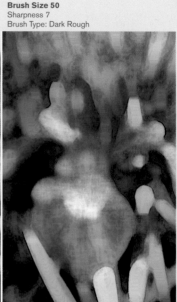

DEFAULT–BRUSH TYPE: WIDE SHARP

BRUSH SIZE

Brush Size 20
Sharpness 7
Brush Type: Wide Sharp

Brush Size 50
Sharpness 7
Brush Type: Wide Sharp

DEFAULT

Paint Daubs

Brush Size   8

Sharpness   7

Brush Type: Simple

FILTER SETTING PARAMETERS

Brush Size	Min **1**	Max **50**
Sharpness	Min **0**	Max **40**

SHARPNESS

Brush Size 8
Sharpness 40
Brush Type: Dark Rough

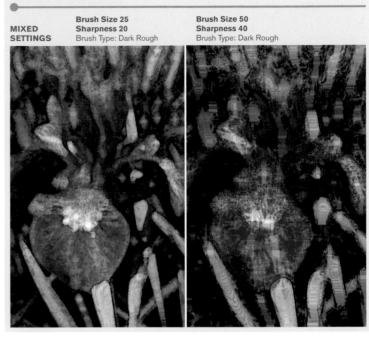

MIXED SETTINGS

Brush Size 25
Sharpness 20
Brush Type: Dark Rough

Brush Size 50
Sharpness 40
Brush Type: Dark Rough

SHARPNESS

Brush Size 8
Sharpness 40
Brush Type: Wide Sharp

MIXED SETTINGS

Brush Size 25
Sharpness 20
Brush Type: Wide Sharp

Brush Size 50
Sharpness 40
Brush Type: Wide Sharp

PAINT DAUBS
WIDE BLURRY/SPARKLE

DEFAULT–BRUSH TYPE: WIDE BLURRY

| **BRUSH SIZE** | **Brush Size 20**
Sharpness 7
Brush Type: Wide Blurry | **Brush Size 50**
Sharpness 7
Brush Type: Wide Blurry |

DEFAULT–BRUSH TYPE: SPARKLE

| **BRUSH SIZE** | **Brush Size 20**
Sharpness 7
Brush Type: Sparkle | **Brush Size 50**
Sharpness 7
Brush Type: Sparkle |

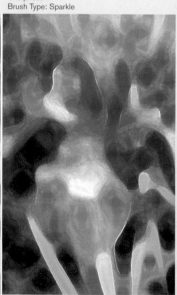

DEFAULT

Paint Daubs	
Brush Size	8
Sharpness	7
Brush Type:	Simple

FILTER SETTING PARAMETERS

Brush Size	Min	1	Max	50
Sharpness	Min	0	Max	40

SHARPNESS
Brush Size 8
Sharpness 40
Brush Type: Wide Blurry

MIXED SETTINGS

Brush Size 25
Sharpness 20
Brush Type: Wide Blurry

Brush Size 50
Sharpness 40
Brush Type: Wide Blurry

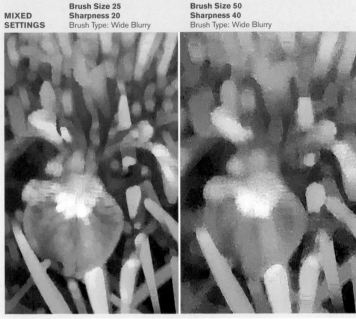

SHARPNESS
Brush Size 8
Sharpness 40
Brush Type: Sparkle

MIXED SETTINGS

Brush Size 25
Sharpness 20
Brush Type: Sparkle

Brush Size 50
Sharpness 40
Brush Type: Sparkle

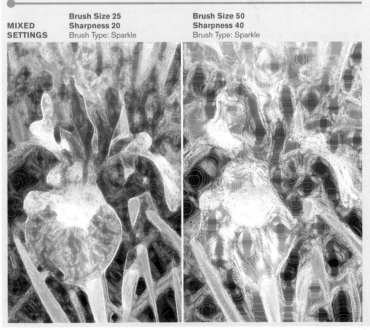

INTRODUCING PALETTE KNIFE

The Palette Knife filter gives the impression of paint applied in patches or swathes. It does this by creating areas of similarly colored pixels, mimicking the use of a palette or painting knife. Although it lacks the texture and varying depth of the real application of the technique, some effective painterly looks can emerge.

ORIGINAL IMAGE

DEFAULT PALETTE KNIFE
Much of the detail of the original image (above) is gone, replaced with smeared blotches of color.

Settings
Stroke Size 25
Stroke Detail 3
Softness 0

BROADER SWEEPS
Setting maximum Stroke Size, the patches of color grow larger, losing more detail.

Settings
Stroke Size 50
Stroke Detail 3
Softness 0

DEFAULT

Palette Knife

Stroke Size   25

Stroke Detail   3

Softness   0

FILTER SETTING PARAMETERS

Stroke Size	Min **1**	Max **50**
Stroke Detail	Min **1**	Max **3**
Softness	Min **0**	Max **10**

ORIGINAL IMAGE

MORE SUBTLE EFFECTS
Keeping more detail can result in a more subtle painterly look. Both of these images still have the leaf vein detail visible, but the filter has also added more contrast.

Settings
Stroke Size 15
Stroke Detail 3
Softness 10

Settings
Stroke Size 8
Stroke Detail 1
Softness 0

IMPRESSIONISTIC
The image on the left looks almost impressionistic, with the details blurred but not yet abstract.

ORIGINAL IMAGE

TRANSLUCENT
This image has a much higher Stroke Size than the image on the far left, which loses the detail as the colors bleed into one another.

Settings
Stroke Size 45
Stroke Detail 3
Softness 0

Settings
Stroke Size 15
Stroke Detail 2
Softness 0

PALETTE KNIFE

DEFAULT

STROKE SIZE	**Stroke Size 10** Stroke Detail 3 Softness 0	**Stroke Size 35** Stroke Detail 3 Softness 0

MIXED SETTINGS	**Stroke Size 10** **Stroke Detail 1** Softness 0	**Stroke Size 35** **Stroke Detail 1** Softness 0	**Stroke Size 50** **Stroke Detail 1** Softness 0

DEFAULT

Palette Knife	⬍
Stroke Size	25
Stroke Detail	3
Softness	0

FILTER SETTING PARAMETERS

Stroke Size	Min **1**	Max **50**
Stroke Detail	Min **1**	Max **3**
Softness	Min **0**	Max **10**

STROKE DETAIL

Stroke Size 25
Stroke Detail 1
Softness 0

Stroke Size 25
Stroke Detail 2
Softness 0

SOFTNESS

Stroke Size 25
Stroke Detail 3
Softness 10

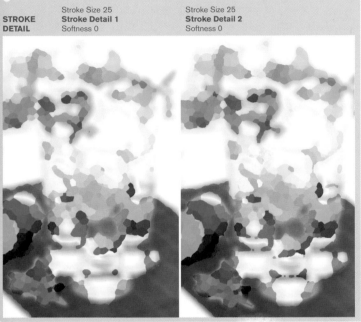

Stroke Size 4
Stroke Detail 1
Softness 0

Stroke Size 15
Stroke Detail 2
Softness 0

Stroke Size 40
Stroke Detail 2
Softness 10

INTRODUCING PLASTIC WRAP

Plastic Wrap is designed to give the impression of a plastic blister wrap covering by creating black and white areas in the shadows of the image. It is very useful for creating a shiny effect on objects.

ORIGINAL IMAGE

DEFAULT PLASTIC WRAP
The filter applied with default settings creates more contrasted edges with opaque highlights.

Settings
Highlight Strength 15
Detail 9
Smoothness 7

MORE DETAIL
With the Highlight Strength reduced and the Detail increased, the effect is more subtle, with fewer opaque areas.

Settings
Highlight Strength 10
Detail 12
Smoothness 5

DEFAULT

Plastic Wrap	⬍
Highlight Strength	15
Detail	9
Smoothness	7

FILTER SETTING PARAMETERS

Highlight Strength Min **0**		Max **20**
Detail	Min **1**	Max **15**
Smoothness	Min **1**	Max **15**

OPAQUE COVERING
Left: With a much higher Highlight Strength, less Detail, and increased Smoothness, the effect is much more opaque.

Settings
Highlight Strength 17
Detail 6
Smoothness 15

ORIGINAL IMAGE

CREATING SHINE
Right: You can use the filter to add a shiny quality to objects in an image with a lower Highlight Strength.

Settings
Highlight Strength 5
Detail 11
Smoothness 5

Settings
Highlight Strength 20
Detail 1
Smoothness 15

ORIGINAL IMAGE

GENTLE GLOW OR SHARP HIGHLIGHT
Far left: The veins of the flowers are still visible in this image, which has a high Detail setting, the filter creating a gentle glow and a softening of the image. **Left:** This image is very different, with a strong highlight around the edges of the flowers, but less detail.

Settings
Highlight Strength 9
Detail 15
Smoothness 15

PLASTIC WRAP

DEFAULT

HIGHLIGHT STRENGTH

Highlight Strength 3
Detail 9
Smoothness 7

Highlight Strength 7
Detail 9
Smoothness 7

Highlight Strength 15
Detail 5
Smoothness 7

Highlight Strength 15
Detail 12
Smoothness 7

Highlight Strength 15
Detail 15
Smoothness 7

Highlight Strength 15
Detail 9
Smoothness 15

MIXED SETTINGS

Highlight Strength 5
Detail 2
Smoothness 7

Highlight Strength 9
Detail 5
Smoothness 2

DEFAULT

Plastic Wrap

Highlight Strength 15

Detail 9

Smoothness 7

FILTER SETTING PARAMETERS

Highlight Strength	Min **0**	Max **20**
Detail	Min **1**	Max **15**
Smoothness	Min **1**	Max **15**

Highlight Strength 11
Detail 9
Smoothness 7

Highlight Strength 20
Detail 9
Smoothness 7

DETAIL

Highlight Strength 15
Detail 1
Smoothness 7

SMOOTHNESS

Highlight Strength 15
Detail 9
Smoothness 1

Highlight Strength 15
Detail 9
Smoothness 4

Highlight Strength 15
Detail 9
Smoothness 11

Highlight Strength 20
Detail 12
Smoothness 5

Highlight Strength 20
Detail 15
Smoothness 3

Highlight Strength 10
Detail 5
Smoothness 15

INTRODUCING POSTER EDGES

When you apply this filter, you'll find the edges in your image are highlighted with dark lines of varying thicknesses and intensity depending on the Edge Thickness and Edge Intensity settings. The Posterization setting can produce blocks of colors.

ORIGINAL IMAGE

DEFAULT POSTER EDGES
The edges are emphasized in black and the image has a grainy effect.

Settings
Edge Thickness 2
Edge Intensity 1
Posterization 2

CINEMA POSTER EFFECT
The image has fewer colors with the Posterization setting so low, and the low Edge Intensity creates a much less grainy effect.

Settings
Edge Thickness 5
Edge Intensity 0
Posterization 1

DEFAULT

Poster Edges
Edge Thickness — 2
Edge Intensity — 1
Posterization — 2

FILTER SETTING PARAMETERS

Edge Thickness	Min	0	Max	10
Edge Intensity	Min	0	Max	10
Posterization	Min	0	Max	6

TRACING LINES
The veins of the orchid are highlighted with black lines.

Settings
Edge Thickness 10
Edge Intensity 5
Posterization 6

ORIGINAL IMAGE

ADDING GRAININESS
With the Edge Intensity at its maximum, all the tiny details are turned into a grainy effect.

Settings
Edge Thickness 5
Edge Intensity 10
Posterization 3

ORIGINAL IMAGE

STRIKING DIFFERENCES
The high setting for Edge Intensity for the image on the left, combined with no Edge Thickness, emphasizes the fur and all the flecks in the eyes. In contrast, the image on the right has no Edge Intensity and a high Edge Thickness, giving far fewer and much thicker black lines.

Settings
Edge Thickness 0
Edge Intensity 10
Posterization 1

Settings
Edge Thickness 10
Edge Intensity 0
Posterization 0

POSTER EDGES

DEFAULT

EDGE THICKNESS

Edge Thickness 0
Edge Intensity 1
Posterization 2

Edge Thickness 6
Edge Intensity 1
Posterization 2

Edge Thickness 2
Edge Intensity 10
Posterization 2

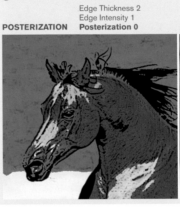

POSTERIZATION

Edge Thickness 2
Edge Intensity 1
Posterization 0

Edge Thickness 2
Edge Intensity 1
Posterization 4

Edge Thickness 10
Edge Intensity 0
Posterization 2

Edge Thickness 0
Edge Intensity 10
Posterization 2

Edge Thickness 10
Edge Intensity 10
Posterization 2

DEFAULT

Poster Edges

Edge Thickness 2

Edge Intensity 1

Posterization 2

FILTER SETTING PARAMETERS

Edge Thickness   Min **0**   Max **10**

Edge Intensity   Min **0**   Max **10**

Posterization   Min **0**   Max **6**

Edge Thickness 10
Edge Intensity 1
Posterization 2

EDGE INTENSITY

Edge Thickness 2
Edge Intensity 0
Posterization 2

Edge Thickness 2
Edge Intensity 5
Posterization 2

Edge Thickness 2
Edge Intensity 1
Posterization 6

MIXED SETTINGS

Edge Thickness 0
Edge Intensity 0
Posterization 2

Edge Thickness 4
Edge Intensity 4
Posterization 2

Edge Thickness 10
Edge Intensity 0
Posterization 0

Edge Thickness 0
Edge Intensity 10
Posterization 6

Edge Thickness 10
Edge Intensity 1
Posterization 6

INTRODUCING ROUGH PASTELS

The Rough Pastels filter creates diagonal lines (by slightly offsetting the whole image) that are texturized according to the Texture you have selected. The lines are controlled by the Stroke Length and Stroke Detail settings, and there are also settings to determine the strength of the texture effect. You can load your own textures to apply with the filter.

ORIGINAL IMAGE

DEFAULT ROUGH PASTELS
Intended to change a photograph so it looks as though it has been drawn with pastels, the filter's impact on this image isn't entirely convincing, but it is still useful if you want to move toward an illustrative effect.

Settings
Stroke Length 6
Stroke Detail 4
Texture: Canvas
Scaling 100%
Relief 20

LONGER PASTEL STROKES
By increasing the Stroke Length and the Stroke Detail, the effect is more pronounced.

Settings
Stroke Length 30
Stroke Detail 7
Texture: Canvas
Scaling 100%
Relief 20

DEFAULT

Rough Pastels		
Stroke Length	6	
Stroke Detail	4	
Texture	Canvas	
Scaling	100 %	
Relief	20	
Light	Bottom	
Invert		

FILTER SETTING PARAMETERS

Stroke Length	Min **0**	Max **40**
Stroke Detail	Min **1**	Max **20**

ORIGINAL IMAGE

PASTEL ON SANDSTONE
Right: Using the Sandstone Texture with a higher Stroke Detail setting creates a striking effect.

Settings
Stroke Length 3
Stroke Detail 12
Texture: Sandstone
Scaling 55%
Relief 30

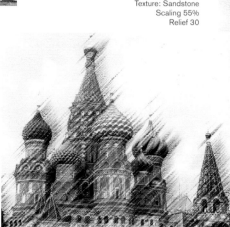

PASTEL ON BURLAP
Left: A very high Stroke Length and Stroke Detail setting, combined with a low Relief and Scaling value for the texture, creates pronounced diagonal lines.

Settings
Stroke Length 40
Stroke Detail 14
Texture: Burlap
Scaling 50%
Relief 15

Settings
Stroke Length 5
Stroke Detail 10
Texture: Brick
Scaling 200%
Relief 10

ORIGINAL IMAGE

HORIZONTAL LINES
Far left: The Brick Texture applied at a high Scaling and with low Relief generates this strange horizontal-lined effect.

EMPHASIZING TEXTURE
Left: The pastel effect is reduced to a minimum with the low Stroke Length and Stroke Detail settings. The higher texture settings (Scaling and Relief) emphasize the "ground."

Settings
Stroke Length 1
Stroke Detail 2
Texture: Burlap
Scaling 120%
Relief 30

ROUGH PASTELS
CANVAS

DEFAULT CANVAS TEXTURE

STROKE LENGTH   **Stroke Length 12**
Stroke Detail 4

STROKE DETAIL   Stroke Length 6
Stroke Detail 1

Stroke Length 6
Stroke Detail 8

MIXED SETTINGS   **Stroke Length 0**
Stroke Detail 5

Stroke Length 12
Stroke Detail 15

DEFAULT

Rough Pastels

Stroke Length   6

Stroke Detail   4

Texture: Canvas

FILTER SETTING PARAMETERS

Stroke Length	Min 0	Max 40
Stroke Detail	Min 1	Max 20

These images show the default Canvas Texture with variations in the Stroke Length and Stroke Detail settings. See pages 80–81 for variations in Texture settings.

Stroke Length 20
Stroke Detail 4

Stroke Length 40
Stroke Detail 4

Stroke Length 6
Stroke Detail 14

Stroke Length 6
Stroke Detail 20

Stroke Length 20
Stroke Detail 10

Stroke Length 40
Stroke Detail 20

ROUGH PASTELS
CANVAS (CONTINUED)

TEXTURE SETTINGS

Scaling 50%
Relief 20
Light: Top

Scaling 150%
Relief 20
Light: Top

MIXED SETTINGS

Stroke Length 6
Stroke Detail 4

Scaling 50%
Relief 10
Light: Top

Stroke Length 5
Stroke Detail 15

Scaling 50%
Relief 30
Light: Top

CANVAS TEXTURE SETTINGS

DEFAULT

Texture: Canvas
Scaling   100 %
Relief   20
Light: Top

FILTER SETTING PARAMETERS

Scaling	Min **50%**	Max **200%**
Relief	Min **0**	Max **50**

These images show variations of the Scaling and Relief Texture settings, and mixed settings of all options.

Scaling 100%
Relief 1
Light: Top

Scaling 100%
Relief 50
Light: Top

Stroke Length 5
Stroke Detail 5

Scaling 200%
Relief 2
Light: Top

Stroke Length 15
Stroke Detail 15

Scaling 115%
Relief 20
Light: Top

ROUGH PASTELS
BRICK

DEFAULT BRICK TEXTURE

STROKE LENGTH   **Stroke Length 12**
Stroke Detail 4

STROKE DETAIL   Stroke Length 6
Stroke Detail 1

Stroke Length 6
Stroke Detail 8

MIXED SETTINGS   Stroke Length 0
Stroke Detail 5

Stroke Length 12
Stroke Detail 15

DEFAULT

FILTER SETTING PARAMETERS

Stroke Length	Min **0**	Max **40**	
Stroke Detail	Min **1**	Max **20**	

These images show Brick Texture with variations in the Stroke Length and Stroke Detail settings. See pages 84–85 for variations in Texture settings.

Stroke Length 20
Stroke Detail 4

Stroke Length 40
Stroke Detail 4

Stroke Length 6
Stroke Detail 14

Stroke Length 6
Stroke Detail 20

Stroke Length 20
Stroke Detail 10

Stroke Length 40
Stroke Detail 20

ROUGH PASTELS
BRICK (CONTINUED)

TEXTURE SETTINGS

Scaling 50%
Relief 20
Light: Top

Scaling 150%
Relief 20
Light: Top

MIXED SETTINGS

Stroke Length 6
Stroke Detail 4

Scaling 50%
Relief 10
Light: Top

Stroke Length 5
Stroke Detail 15

Scaling 50%
Relief 30
Light: Top

**BRICK TEXTURE
SETTINGS**

DEFAULT

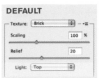

FILTER SETTING PARAMETERS

Scaling	Min **50%**	Max **200%**	
Relief	Min **0**	Max **50**	

These images show variations of the
Scaling and Relief Texture settings,
and mixed settings of all options.

Scaling 100%
Relief 1
Light: Top

Scaling 100%
Relief 50
Light: Top

Stroke Length 5
Stroke Detail 5

Scaling 200%
Relief 2
Light: Top

Stroke Length 15
Stroke Detail 15

Scaling 115%
Relief 20
Light: Top

ROUGH PASTELS
BURLAP

DEFAULT BURLAP TEXTURE

STROKE LENGTH

Stroke Length 12
Stroke Detail 4

STROKE DETAIL

Stroke Length 6
Stroke Detail 1

Stroke Length 6
Stroke Detail 8

MIXED SETTINGS

Stroke Length 0
Stroke Detail 5

Stroke Length 12
Stroke Detail 15

DEFAULT

Rough Pastels	⇕
Stroke Length	6
Stroke Detail	4
Texture: Burlap	⇕

FILTER SETTING PARAMETERS

Stroke Length	Min **0**	Max **40**	
Stroke Detail	Min **1**	Max **20**	

These images show Burlap Texture with variations in the Stroke Length and Stroke Detail settings. See pages 88–89 for variations in Texture settings.

Stroke Length 20
Stroke Detail 4

Stroke Length 40
Stroke Detail 4

Stroke Length 6
Stroke Detail 14

Stroke Length 6
Stroke Detail 20

Stroke Length 20
Stroke Detail 10

Stroke Length 40
Stroke Detail 20

ROUGH PASTELS
BURLAP (CONTINUED)

**TEXTURE
SETTINGS**

Scaling 50%
Relief 20
Light: Top

Scaling 150%
Relief 20
Light: Top

MIXED SETTINGS

Stroke Length 6
Stroke Detail 4

Scaling 50%
Relief 10
Light: Top

Stroke Length 5
Stroke Detail 15

Scaling 50%
Relief 30
Light: Top

BURLAP TEXTURE SETTINGS

DEFAULT

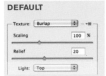

Texture:	Burlap
Scaling	100 %
Relief	20
Light:	Top

FILTER SETTING PARAMETERS

| Scaling | Min **50%** | Max **200%** |
| Relief | Min **0** | Max **50** |

These images show variations of the Scaling and Relief Texture settings, and mixed settings of all options.

Scaling 100%
Relief 1
Light: Top

Scaling 100%
Relief 50
Light: Top

Stroke Length 5
Stroke Detail 5

Scaling 200%
Relief 2
Light: Top

Stroke Length 15
Stroke Detail 15

Scaling 115%
Relief 20
Light: Top

ROUGH PASTELS
SANDSTONE

DEFAULT SANDSTONE TEXTURE

**STROKE
LENGTH**

Stroke Length 12
Stroke Detail 4

**STROKE
DETAIL**

Stroke Length 6
Stroke Detail 1

Stroke Length 6
Stroke Detail 8

**MIXED
SETTINGS**

Stroke Length 0
Stroke Detail 5

Stroke Length 12
Stroke Detail 15

DEFAULT

Rough Pastels	
Stroke Length	6
Stroke Detail	4
Texture:	Sandstone

FILTER SETTING PARAMETERS

Stroke Length	Min **0**	Max **40**
Stroke Detail	Min **1**	Max **20**

These images show Sandstone Texture with variations in the Stroke Length and Stroke Detail settings. See pages 92–93 for variations in Texture settings.

Stroke Length 20
Stroke Detail 4

Stroke Length 40
Stroke Detail 4

Stroke Length 6
Stroke Detail 14

Stroke Length 6
Stroke Detail 20

Stroke Length 20
Stroke Detail 10

Stroke Length 40
Stroke Detail 20

ROUGH PASTELS
SANDSTONE (CONTINUED)

**TEXTURE
SETTINGS**

Scaling 50%
Relief 20
Light: Top

Scaling 150%
Relief 20
Light: Top

MIXED SETTINGS

Stroke Length 6
Stroke Detail 4

Scaling 50%
Relief 10
Light: Top

Stroke Length 5
Stroke Detail 15

Scaling 50%
Relief 30
Light: Top

SANDSTONE TEXTURE SETTINGS

DEFAULT

FILTER SETTING PARAMETERS

Scaling	Min **50%**	Max **200%**
Relief	Min **0**	Max **50**

These images show variations of the Scaling and Relief Texture settings, and mixed settings of all options.

Scaling 100%
Relief 1
Light: Top

Scaling 100%
Relief 50
Light: Top

Stroke Length 5
Stroke Detail 5

Scaling 200%
Relief 2
Light: Top

Stroke Length 5
Stroke Detail 5

Scaling 115%
Relief 20
Light: Top

INTRODUCING SMUDGE STICK

Use the Smudge Stick filter to apply a burnished pastel effect to a photograph. The filter smears darker pixels, and blurs and brightens lighter areas. Increasing the Stroke Length makes the diagonal smears longer and more pronounced, while the Highlight Area only has an effect in combination with the Intensity.

ORIGINAL IMAGE

DEFAULT SMUDGE STICK
This image has a smudged pastel look. A texture could be applied using the Texturizer filter.

Settings
Stroke Length 2
Highlight Area 0
Intensity 10

INTENSE CONTRAST
Once the Highlight Area is increased, the whites are blown and the shadows become darker, enhancing the overall contrast.

Settings
Stroke Length 5
Highlight Area 9
Intensity 5

DEFAULT

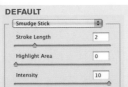

Smudge Stick

Stroke Length   2

Highlight Area   0

Intensity   10

FILTER SETTING PARAMETERS

Stroke Length	Min **0**	Max **10**
Highlight Area	Min **0**	Max **20**
Intensity	Min **0**	Max **10**

STILL LIFE
With a low Stroke Length value, detail is retained.

Settings
Stroke Length 1
Highlight Area 3
Intensity 6

ORIGINAL IMAGE

BRIGHTENED STILL LIFE
The Highlight Area value has been increased to its maximum, giving much more detail to the shadow areas in the image.

Settings
Stroke Length 1
Highlight Area 20
Intensity 5

Settings
Stroke Length 10
Highlight Area 9
Intensity 2

ORIGINAL IMAGE

SHARPENING AND SOFTENING
These two images demonstrate how the filter can be used to different effect: bringing out the detail in the image on the far left, highlighting the fluffy cacti, and softening and dimming the detail in the image on the left.

Settings
Stroke Length 0
Highlight Area 15
Intensity 7

SMUDGE STICK

DEFAULT

STROKE LENGTH

Stroke Length 0	**Stroke Length 10**
Highlight Area 0	Highlight Area 0
Intensity 10	Intensity 10

INTENSITY

Stroke Length 2
Highlight Area 0
Intensity 0

MIXED SETTINGS

Stroke Length 5	**Stroke Length 5**
Highlight Area 5	**Highlight Area 20**
Intensity 10	Intensity 10

DEFAULT

Smudge Stick	
Stroke Length	2
Highlight Area	0
Intensity	10

FILTER SETTING PARAMETERS

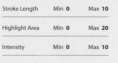

Stroke Length	Min 0	Max 10
Highlight Area	Min 0	Max 20
Intensity	Min 0	Max 10

HIGHLIGHT AREA

Stroke Length 2
Highlight Area 7
Intensity 10

Stroke Length 2
Highlight Area 14
Intensity 10

Stroke Length 2
Highlight Area 20
Intensity 10

Stroke Length 10
Highlight Area 6
Intensity 10

Stroke Length 10
Highlight Area 12
Intensity 10

Stroke Length 10
Highlight Area 17
Intensity 5

INTRODUCING SPONGE

The Sponge filter replicates the effect of rolling a sponge over a painted illustration to give it texture. To achieve this, Photoshop applies a random pattern to the image. The Brush Size increases the size of the pattern while the Definition setting increases the contrast of the pattern. Increasing the Smoothness setting blurs the image.

ORIGINAL IMAGE

DEFAULT SPONGE
The Sponge filter blurs the image slightly to give it a painterly effect and adds a patterned texture.

Settings
Brush Size 2
Definition 12
Smoothness 5

MINIMAL DETAIL
Reducing Definition to its minimum and increasing Smoothness to its near maximum renders a very low-detail image.

Settings
Brush Size 2
Definition 0
Smoothness 14

DEFAULT

Sponge		
Brush Size	2	
Definition	12	
Smoothness	5	

FILTER SETTING PARAMETERS

Brush Size	Min 0	Max 10
Definition	Min 0	Max 25
Smoothness	Min 1	Max 15

HIGH-DETAIL IMAGE

This photograph already contains a high amount of detail (see right), so the texture of the sponge is less apparent. All the values are kept low in the image on the left but increased substantially in the image below.

ORIGINAL IMAGE

Settings
Brush Size 3
Definition 0
Smoothness 2

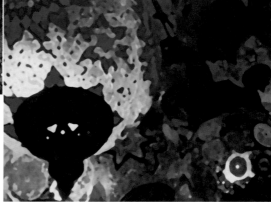

Settings
Brush Size 9
Definition 9
Smoothness 9

ADDING TEXTURE

The plain background of this still life shows how the Sponge filter can add texture to a flat background. The Brush Size and Definition settings create very different textured effects.

ORIGINAL IMAGE

Settings
Brush Size 3
Definition 6
Smoothness 1

Settings
Brush Size 10
Definition 25
Smoothness 1

SPONGE

DEFAULT

BRUSH SIZE

Brush Size 0
Definition 12
Smoothness 5

Brush Size 6
Definition 12
Smoothness 5

Brush Size 2
Definition 18
Smoothness 5

Brush Size 2
Definition 25
Smoothness 5

SMOOTHNESS

Brush Size 2
Definition 12
Smoothness 1

Brush Size 5
Definition 0
Smoothness 5

Brush Size 5
Definition 5
Smoothness 5

Brush Size 0
Definition 5
Smoothness 5

DEFAULT

Sponge	
Brush Size	2
Definition	12
Smoothness	5

FILTER SETTING PARAMETERS

Brush Size	Min **0**	Max **10**
Definition	Min **0**	Max **25**
Smoothness	Min **1**	Max **15**

Brush Size 10
Definition 12
Smoothness 5

DEFINITION

Brush Size 2
Definition 0
Smoothness 5

Brush Size 2
Definition 6
Smoothness 5

Brush Size 2
Definition 12
Smoothness 10

Brush Size 2
Definition 12
Smoothness 15

MIXED SETTINGS

Brush Size 0
Definition 0
Smoothness 5

Brush Size 10
Definition 0
Smoothness 5

Brush Size 0
Definition 25
Smoothness 5

Brush Size 10
Definition 0
Smoothness 15

INTRODUCING UNDERPAINTING

This filter mimics the effect of an artist's underpainting, taking the basic details of the image and applying a texture to it. Increasing the Brush Size setting loses detail from the image, and you can determine the strength of the Texture application by adjusting the Texture Coverage setting.

ORIGINAL IMAGE

DEFAULT UNDERPAINTING
With the default settings applied, the image is ready for the next layer of paint, which could take the form of another filter.

Settings
Brush Size 6
Texture Coverage 16
Texture: Canvas
Scaling 100%
Relief 4
Light: Top

STRONG TEXTURE
Using both a big Brush Size and a higher Texture Relief setting using Burlap, the image becomes a more general representation of the original, with a strong burlap texture.

Settings
Brush Size 40
Texture Coverage 16
Texture: Burlap
Scaling 75%
Relief 10
Light: Top

DEFAULT

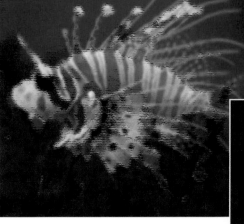

FILTER SETTING PARAMETERS

Brush Size	Min **0**	Max **40**
Texture Coverage	Min **0**	Max **40**

SUBTLE CANVAS
The Canvas Texture is highlighted around the edges with a low Texture Coverage value.

Settings
Brush Size 20
Texture Coverage 5
Texture: Canvas
Scaling 200%
Relief 30
Light: Top

ORIGINAL IMAGE

SANDSTONE TEXTURE
With a Brush Size of 0 and the maximum Texture Coverage, there is more detail combined with a soft sandstone texture.

Settings
Brush Size 0
Texture Coverage 40
Texture: Sandstone
Scaling 150%
Relief 10
Light: Top

ORIGINAL IMAGE

SHARP TEXTURE
The Brick Texture creates areas of strongly textured detail.

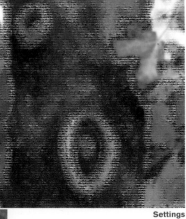

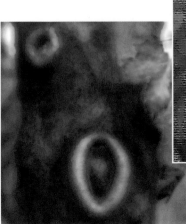

SOFT UNDERPAINTING
Using a lower Brush Size value and very high Texture Coverage gives this soft-focus effect.

Settings
Brush Size 9
Texture Coverage 40
Texture: Burlap
Scaling 65%
Relief 0
Light: Top

Settings
Brush Size 25
Texture Coverage 36
Texture: Brick
Scaling 110%
Relief 50
Light: Top

UNDERPAINTING
CANVAS

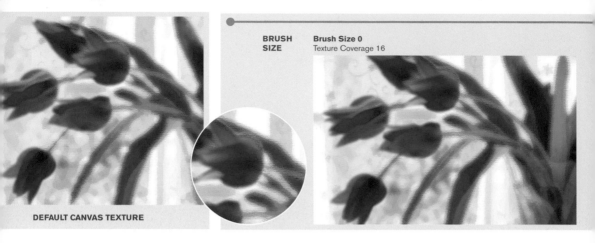

BRUSH SIZE

Brush Size 0
Texture Coverage 16

DEFAULT CANVAS TEXTURE

TEXTURE COVERAGE

Brush Size 6
Texture Coverage 0

Brush Size 6
Texture Coverage 25

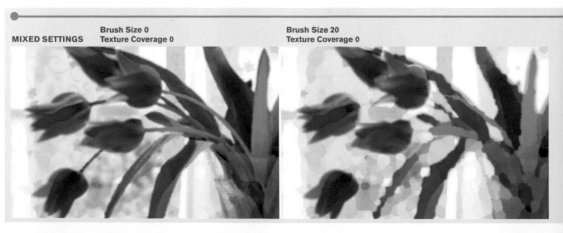

MIXED SETTINGS

Brush Size 0
Texture Coverage 0

Brush Size 20
Texture Coverage 0

DEFAULT

Underpainting

Brush Size 6

Texture Coverage 16

Texture: Canvas

FILTER SETTING PARAMETERS

Brush Size	Min **0**	Max **40**	
Texture Coverage	Min **0**	Max **40**	

These images show the default Underpainting Texture with variations in Brush Size and Texture Coverage settings. See pages 106–107 for variations in Texture settings.

Brush Size 20
Texture Coverage 16

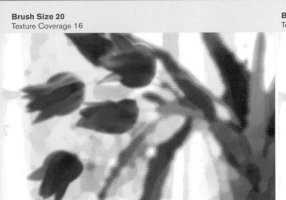

Brush Size 40
Texture Coverage 16

Brush Size 6
Texture Coverage 30

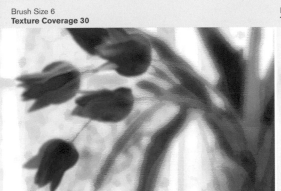

Brush Size 6
Texture Coverage 40

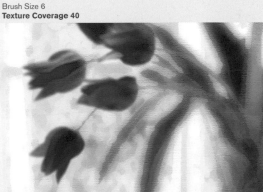

Brush Size 0
Texture Coverage 40

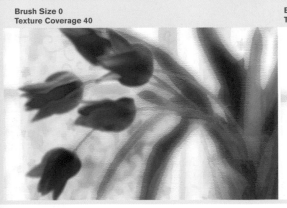

Brush Size 20
Texture Coverage 40

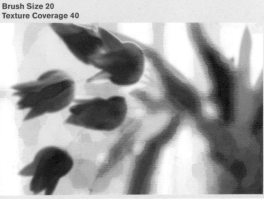

UNDERPAINTING
CANVAS (CONTINUED)

**TEXTURE
SETTINGS**

Scaling 50%
Relief 4
Light: Top

Scaling 200%
Relief 4
Light: Top

MIXED SETTINGS

Brush Size 6
Texture Coverage 16

Scaling 200%
Relief 50
Light: Top

Brush Size 30
Texture Coverage 5

Scaling 100%
Relief 30
Light: Top

CANVAS TEXTURE SETTINGS

DEFAULT

FILTER SETTING PARAMETERS

Scaling	Min **50%**	Max **200%**
Relief	Min **0**	Max **50**

These images show variations of the Scaling and Relief settings, and mixed settings of all options.

Scaling 100%
Relief 25
Light: Top

Scaling 100%
Relief 50
Light: Top

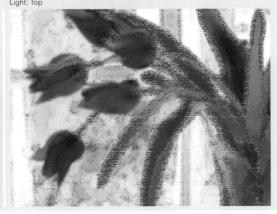

Brush Size 20
Texture Coverage 20

Scaling 150%
Relief 20
Light: Top

Brush Size 30
Texture Coverage 30

Scaling 200%
Relief 50
Light: Top

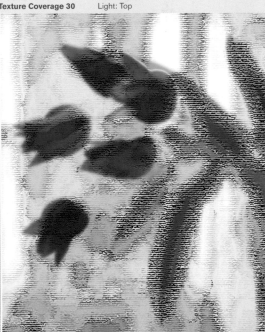

UNDERPAINTING
BRICK

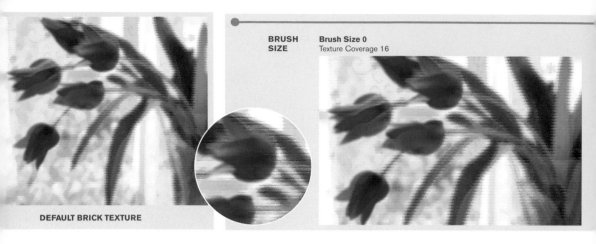

DEFAULT BRICK TEXTURE

BRUSH SIZE

Brush Size 0
Texture Coverage 16

TEXTURE COVERAGE

Brush Size 6
Texture Coverage 0

Brush Size 6
Texture Coverage 25

MIXED SETTINGS

Brush Size 0
Texture Coverage 0

Brush Size 20
Texture Coverage 0

DEFAULT

Underpainting

Brush Size   6

Texture Coverage   16

Texture: Brick

FILTER SETTING PARAMETERS

Brush Size   Min 0   Max 40

Texture Coverage   Min 0   Max 40

These images show Brick Texture with variations in Brush Size and Texture Coverage settings. See pages 110–111 for variations in Texture settings.

Brush Size 20
Texture Coverage 16

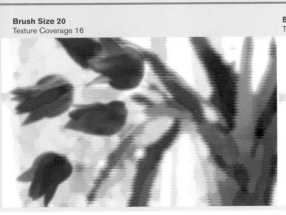

Brush Size 40
Texture Coverage 16

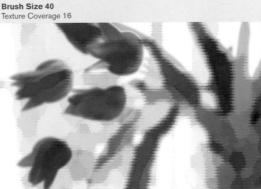

Brush Size 6
Texture Coverage 30

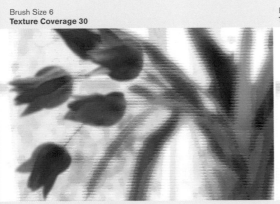

Brush Size 6
Texture Coverage 40

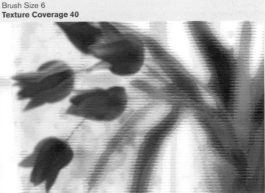

Brush Size 0
Texture Coverage 40

Brush Size 40
Texture Coverage 40

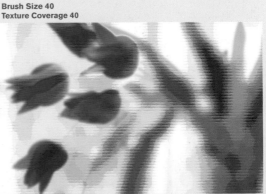

**TEXTURE
SETTINGS**

Scaling 50%
Relief 4
Light: Top

Scaling 200%
Relief 4
Light: Top

MIXED SETTINGS

Brush Size 6
Texture Coverage 16

Scaling 200%
Relief 50
Light: Top

Brush Size 30
Texture Coverage 5

Scaling 100%
Relief 30
Light: Top

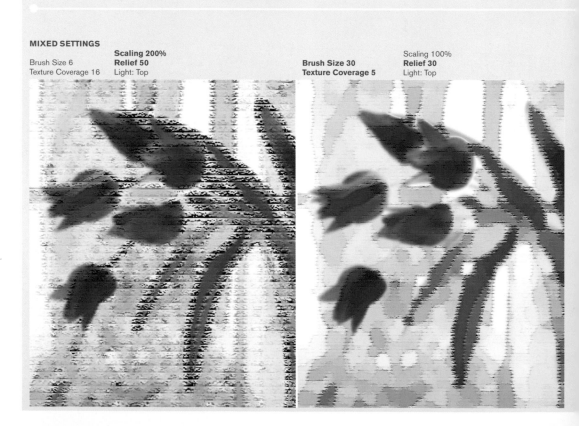

BRICK TEXTURE SETTINGS

DEFAULT

FILTER SETTING PARAMETERS

Scaling	Min **50%**	Max **200%**
Relief	Min **0**	Max **50**

These images show variations of the Scaling and Relief settings, and mixed settings of all options.

Scaling 100%
Relief 25
Light: Top

Scaling 100%
Relief 50
Light: Top

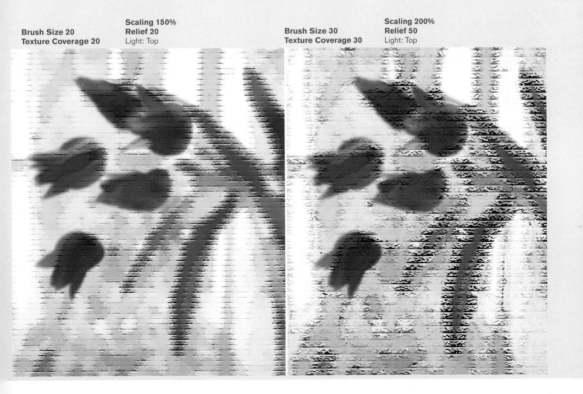

Brush Size 20
Texture Coverage 20

Scaling 150%
Relief 20
Light: Top

Brush Size 30
Texture Coverage 30

Scaling 200%
Relief 50
Light: Top

UNDERPAINTING
BURLAP

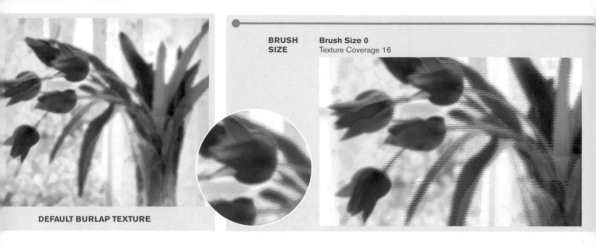

DEFAULT BURLAP TEXTURE

BRUSH SIZE

Brush Size 0
Texture Coverage 16

TEXTURE COVERAGE

Brush Size 6
Texture Coverage 0

Brush Size 6
Texture Coverage 25

MIXED SETTINGS

Brush Size 0
Texture Coverage 0

Brush Size 20
Texture Coverage 0

DEFAULT

Underpainting

Brush Size 6

Texture Coverage 16

Texture: Burlap

FILTER SETTING PARAMETERS

Brush Size	Min **0**	Max **40**
Texture Coverage	Min **0**	Max **40**

These images show Burlap Texture with variations in Brush Size and Texture Coverage settings. See pages 114–115 for variations in Texture settings.

Brush Size 20
Texture Coverage 16

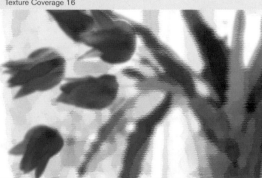

Brush Size 40
Texture Coverage 16

Brush Size 6
Texture Coverage 30

Brush Size 6
Texture Coverage 40

Brush Size 0
Texture Coverage 40

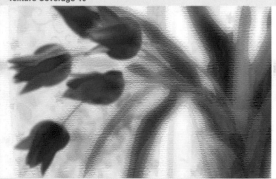

Brush Size 40
Texture Coverage 40

UNDERPAINTING
BURLAP (CONTINUED)

TEXTURE SETTINGS

Scaling 50%
Relief 4
Light: Top

Scaling 200%
Relief 4
Light: Top

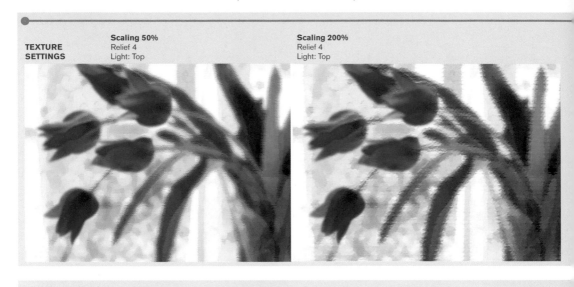

MIXED SETTINGS

Brush Size 6
Texture Coverage 16

Scaling 200%
Relief 50
Light: Top

Brush Size 30
Texture Coverage 5

Scaling 100%
Relief 30
Light: Top

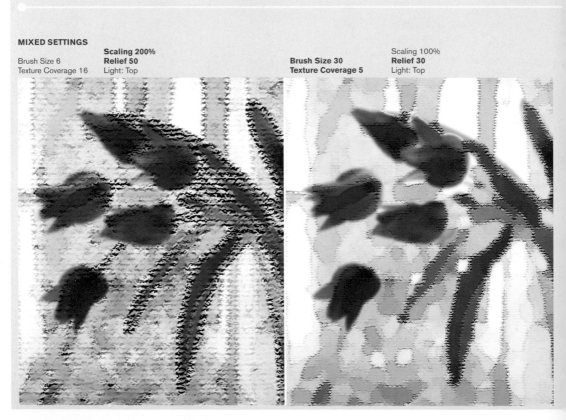

BURLAP TEXTURE SETTINGS

DEFAULT

Texture:	Burlap
Scaling	100 %
Relief	4
Light:	Top
☐ Invert	

FILTER SETTING PARAMETERS

Scaling	Min **50%**	Max **200%**	
Relief	Min **0**	Max **50**	

These images show variations of the Scaling and Relief settings, and mixed settings of all options.

Scaling 100%
Relief 25
Light: Top

Scaling 100%
Relief 50
Light: Top

Brush Size 20
Texture Coverage 20

Scaling 150%
Relief 20
Light: Top

Brush Size 30
Texture Coverage 30

Scaling 200%
Relief 50
Light: Top

UNDERPAINTING
SANDSTONE

DEFAULT SANDSTONE TEXTURE

BRUSH SIZE

Brush Size 0
Texture Coverage 16

TEXTURE COVERAGE

Brush Size 6
Texture Coverage 0

Brush Size 6
Texture Coverage 25

MIXED SETTINGS

Brush Size 0
Texture Coverage 0

Brush Size 20
Texture Coverage 0

DEFAULT

Underpainting

Brush Size   6

Texture Coverage   16

Texture: Sandstone

FILTER SETTING PARAMETERS

Brush Size	Min **0**	Max **40**
Texture Coverage	Min **0**	Max **40**

These images show Sandstone Texture with variations in Brush Size and Texture Coverage settings. See pages 118–119 for variations in Texture settings.

Brush Size 20
Texture Coverage 16

Brush Size 40
Texture Coverage 16

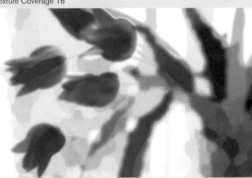

Brush Size 6
Texture Coverage 30

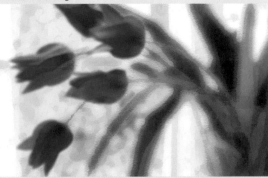

Brush Size 6
Texture Coverage 40

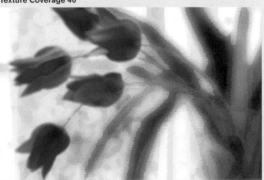

Brush Size 0
Texture Coverage 40

Brush Size 40
Texture Coverage 40

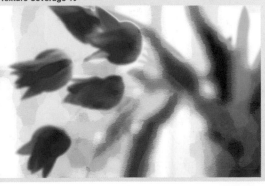

UNDERPAINTING
SANDSTONE (CONTINUED)

**TEXTURE
SETTINGS**

Scaling 50%
Relief 4
Light: Top

Scaling 200%
Relief 4
Light: Top

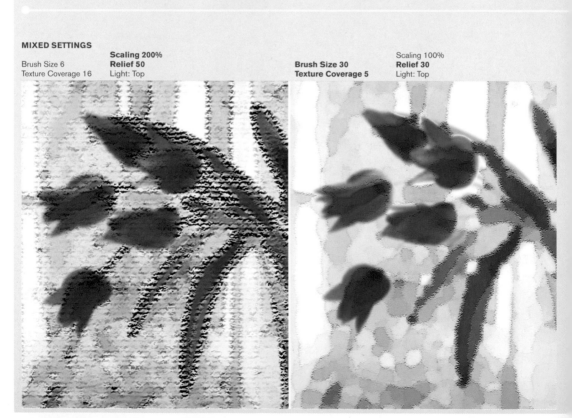

MIXED SETTINGS

Brush Size 6
Texture Coverage 16

Scaling 200%
Relief 50
Light: Top

Brush Size 30
Texture Coverage 5

Scaling 100%
Relief 30
Light: Top

SANDSTONE TEXTURE SETTINGS

DEFAULT

DEFAULT

FILTER SETTING PARAMETERS

Scaling	Min **50%**	Max **200%**
Relief	Min **0**	Max **50**

These images show variations of the Scaling and Relief settings, and mixed settings of all options.

Scaling 100%
Relief 25
Light: Top

Scaling 100%
Relief 50
Light: Top

Brush Size 20
Texture Coverage 20

Scaling 150%
Relief 20
Light: Top

Brush Size 30
Texture Coverage 30

Scaling 200%
Relief 50
Light: Top

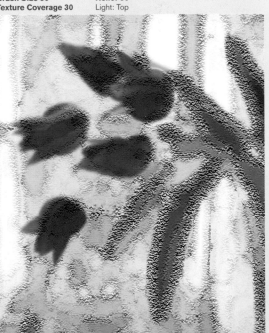

INTRODUCING WATERCOLOR

The difficulty in creating a true watercolor effect from a photograph is that there is no transparency, so the effect of this filter is closer to a gouache painting, similar to watercolor but where the paint is more opaque. As its name implies, the Brush Detail setting increases the amount of detail, while the Shadow Intensity determines the blackness of the shadows. The Texture setting widens the area of bleed of the watercolor effect.

ORIGINAL IMAGE

DEFAULT WATERCOLOR
The darkness generated by the default Shadow Intensity of 1 makes this image too dark. This can be improved by lightening the tonal values before applying the filter.

Settings
Brush Detail 9
Shadow Intensity 1
Texture 1

DELICATE EFFECT
With the Shadow Intensity reduced to 0, the image starts to develop more of a watercolor quality.

Settings
Brush Detail 14
Shadow Intensity 0
Texture 1

DEFAULT

Watercolor

Brush Detail   9

Shadow Intensity   1

Texture   1

FILTER SETTING PARAMETERS

Brush Detail	Min	**1**	Max	**14**
Shadow Intensity	Min	**0**	Max	**10**
Texture	Min	**1**	Max	**3**

DEFINED EDGES
Reducing the Brush Detail creates outlines around the edges that are darkened by Shadow Intensity.

Settings
Brush Detail 2
Shadow Intensity 3
Texture 1

ORIGINAL IMAGE

HIGH TEXTURE
High Brush Detail and Texture values create a contrasting but more detailed effect.

Settings
Brush Detail 9
Shadow Intensity 0
Texture 3

Settings
Brush Detail 4
Shadow Intensity 2
Texture 1

Settings
Brush Detail 12
Shadow Intensity 3
Texture 3

ORIGINAL IMAGE

TEXTURED EFFECTS
This filter can be used to create a textured, painterly effect for your image. These images demonstrate using different settings for varied textures.

WATERCOLOR

DEFAULT

BRUSH DETAIL

Brush Detail 1
Shadow Intensity 1
Texture 1

Brush Detail 14
Shadow Intensity 1
Texture 1

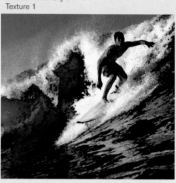

TEXTURE

Brush Detail 9
Shadow Intensity 1
Texture 2

Brush Detail 9
Shadow Intensity 1
Texture 3

MIXED SETTINGS

Brush Detail 1
Shadow Intensity 0
Texture 1

Brush Detail 1
Shadow Intensity 0
Texture 2

Brush Detail 1
Shadow Intensity 3
Texture 2

Brush Detail 5
Shadow Intensity 2
Texture 3

DEFAULT

Watercolor	
Brush Detail	9
Shadow Intensity	1
Texture	1

FILTER SETTING PARAMETERS

Brush Detail	Min **1**	Max **14**
Shadow Intensity	Min **0**	Max **10**
Texture	Min **1**	Max **3**

SHADOW INTENSITY

Brush Detail 9
Shadow Intensity 0
Texture 1

Brush Detail 9
Shadow Intensity 5
Texture 1

Brush Detail 9
Shadow Intensity 10
Texture 1

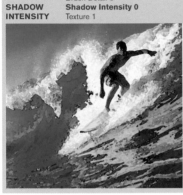

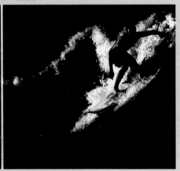

Brush Detail 14
Shadow Intensity 0
Texture 1

Brush Detail 14
Shadow Intensity 5
Texture 1

Brush Detail 14
Shadow Intensity 10
Texture 1

Brush Detail 14
Shadow Intensity 2
Texture 3

Brush Detail 14
Shadow Intensity 4
Texture 3

Brush Detail 14
Shadow Intensity 0
Texture 3

BRUSH STROKES FILTERS

All eight Brush Strokes filters are available through the Filter Gallery. You should find some interesting and perhaps unexpected effects shown in the following pages, for as with the Artistic filters, you may not find that the filter application always matches its name.

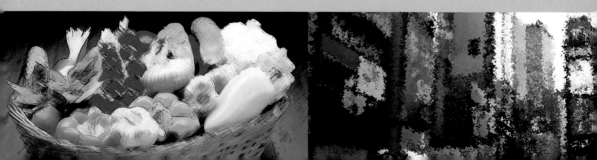

INTRODUCING ACCENTED EDGES

This filter highlights the edges in a photograph by creating black or white lines around them. The settings offer control over the Edge Width, which determines the thickness of the lines; Edge Brightness gradually makes the outlines white, while Smoothness progressively blurs the image.

DEFAULT ACCENTED EDGES
The default settings accent the edges with a highlight and smooth the image overall.

Settings
Edge Width 2
Edge Brightness 38
Smoothness 5

ORIGINAL IMAGE

BLACK OUTLINE
Once the Edge Brightness drops below 25, the outlines become black, creating an effect that is similar to an ink drawing. This is emphasized by keeping the Smoothness to its absolute minimum.

Settings
Edge Width 2
Edge Brightness 23
Smoothness 1

DEFAULT

Accented Edges	
Edge Width	2
Edge Brightness	38
Smoothness	5

FILTER SETTING PARAMETERS

Edge Width	Min **1**	Max **14**
Edge Brightness	Min **0**	Max **50**
Smoothness	Min **1**	Max **15**

DARK AND LIGHT OUTLINES

The only difference between these two images is that the Edge Brightness is set to 0 in the image on the left and to its other extreme of 50 in the image below. A higher Smoothness value reduces the number of outlines.

Settings
Edge Width 1
Edge Brightness 0
Smoothness 9

Settings
Edge Width 1
Edge Brightness 50
Smoothness 9

ORIGINAL IMAGE

DARK EDGE EMPHASIS

The filter settings used for the image to the left result in a gentle black outline of the edges. Changing the Smoothness value produces the effect of a blurred image, as seen below, with contrasting definition around the edges.

ORIGINAL IMAGE

Settings
Edge Width 1
Edge Brightness 13
Smoothness 1

Settings
Edge Width 4
Edge Brightness 21
Smoothness 15

ACCENTED EDGES

DEFAULT

EDGE WIDTH

Edge Width 6
Edge Brightness 38
Smoothness 5

Edge Width 10
Edge Brightness 38
Smoothness 5

Edge Width 2
Edge Brightness 25
Smoothness 5

Edge Width 2
Edge Brightness 50
Smoothness 5

SMOOTHNESS

Edge Width 2
Edge Brightness 38
Smoothness 1

Edge Width 14
Edge Brightness 32
Smoothness 1

Edge Width 2
Edge Brightness 20
Smoothness 5

Edge Width 1
Edge Brightness 50
Smoothness 3

DEFAULT

Accented Edges

Edge Width   2

Edge Brightness   38

Smoothness   5

FILTER SETTING PARAMETERS

Edge Width	Min **1**	Max **14**
Edge Brightness	Min **0**	Max **50**
Smoothness	Min **1**	Max **15**

Edge Width 14
Edge Brightness 38
Smoothness 5

EDGE BRIGHTNESS
Edge Width 2
Edge Brightness 0
Smoothness 5

Edge Width 2
Edge Brightness 10
Smoothness 5

Edge Width 2
Edge Brightness 38
Smoothness 10

Edge Width 2
Edge Brightness 38
Smoothness 15

MIXED SETTINGS
Edge Width 5
Edge Brightness 18
Smoothness 14

Edge Width 2
Edge Brightness 0
Smoothness 4

Edge Width 1
Edge Brightness 10
Smoothness 15

Edge Width 14
Edge Brightness 50
Smoothness 15

INTRODUCING ANGLED STROKES

The effect of this filter is similar to that of a Motion Blur filter (see pages 346): diagonal lines are created, with lighter lines going in the opposite direction to the darker lines. The relative strength of the lines is controlled by Direction Balance. The Stroke Length, as it implies, determines how long the strokes are, and the Sharpness setting creates more defined lines. Bear in mind that the Background Color has an effect on the color of the diagonal lines.

ORIGINAL IMAGE

DEFAULT ANGLED STROKES
The detail in the image is blurred.
Notice how the lighter lines are
angled in a different direction to
the darker lines.

Settings
Direction Balance 50
Stroke Length 15
Sharpness 3

SHARP-ANGLED LINES
Changing the Direction Balance
to 0 makes all the lines run in the
same direction.

Settings
Direction Balance 0
Stroke Length 15
Sharpness 3

DEFAULT

Angled Strokes

Direction Balance	50
Stroke Length	15
Sharpness	3

FILTER SETTING PARAMETERS

Direction Balance	Min 0	Max 100
Stroke Length	Min 3	Max 50
Sharpness	Min 0	Max 10

ENHANCING CONTRAST

With a low value for Stroke Length, and by maximizing Sharpness, a sharper contrast appears along the edges.

Settings
Direction Balance 90
Stroke Length 4
Sharpness 10

ORIGINAL IMAGE

CREATING A SOFTER IMAGE

Most of the detail has been softened by increasing the Stroke Length and minimizing Sharpness.

Settings
Direction Balance 30
Stroke Length 25
Sharpness 0

ABSTRACT EFFECT

Left: With the same settings as were applied to the bamboo (above right), this detailed harbor village develops an abstract look.

ORIGINAL IMAGE

SHARPLY HASHED EFFECT

With fairly short strokes and a high degree of sharpness, the image retains its detail and the hashing of the angled strokes is attractive.

Settings
Direction Balance 25
Stroke Length 7
Sharpness 10

Settings
Direction Balance 30
Stroke Length 25
Sharpness 0

ANGLED STROKES

DEFAULT

DIRECTION BALANCE

Direction Balance 0
Stroke Length 15
Sharpness 3

Direction Balance 100
Stroke Length 15
Sharpness 3

Direction Balance 50
Stroke Length 15
Sharpness 6

Direction Balance 50
Stroke Length 15
Sharpness 10

MIXED SETTINGS

Direction Balance 0
Stroke Length 3
Sharpness 0

DEFAULT

Angled Strokes

Direction Balance	50
Stroke Length	15
Sharpness	3

FILTER SETTING PARAMETERS

Direction Balance	Min **0**	Max **100**
Stroke Length	Min **3**	Max **50**
Sharpness	Min **0**	Max **10**

STROKE LENGTH
Direction Balance 50
Stroke Length 30
Sharpness 3

Direction Balance 50
Stroke Length 50
Sharpness 3

SHARPNESS
Direction Balance 50
Stroke Length 15
Sharpness 0

Direction Balance 0
Stroke Length 15
Sharpness 10

Direction Balance 20
Stroke Length 50
Sharpness 10

Direction Balance 100
Stroke Length 50
Sharpness 10

INTRODUCING CROSSHATCH

Designed to mimic artistic crosshatching, this filter creates diagonal lines that are drawn equally in both directions. Unlike crosshatching, though, the lines pick up the underlying color of the image. The settings are straightforward—the Stroke Length determines how long each stroke is, the Sharpness defines how sharp the strokes are, and the Strength sets the number of crosshatches.

ORIGINAL IMAGE

DEFAULT CROSSHATCH
The settings are all kept low for the default shown here, which creates a subtle but discernible effect.

Settings
Stroke Length 9
Sharpness 6
Strength 1

ADDING TEXTURE
Increasing the Strength to 3 creates a much stronger effect that provides greater texture.

Settings
Stroke Length 6
Sharpness 5
Strength 3

DEFAULT

DEFAULT		FILTER SETTING PARAMETERS		
Crosshatch				
Stroke Length	9	Stroke Length	Min **3**	Max **50**
Sharpness	6	Sharpness	Min **0**	Max **20**
Strength	1	Strength	Min **1**	Max **3**

DEFINED EDGES
A higher Stroke Length means that more detail is lost as the edges become less defined. The Strength of 2 makes the crosshatching more pronounced as well.

Settings
Stroke Length 30
Sharpness 6
Strength 2

ORIGINAL IMAGE

SHORT CROSSHATCH
The shorter crosshatch texture defines the edges by using Sharpness to enhance the contrast.

Settings
Stroke Length 10
Sharpness 15
Strength 1

HIGH DEFINITION
Far left: The crosshatch texture is barely visible with these settings, which have generated a defined image with heightened contrast.

SOFT EFFECT
Left: Despite using a Strength of 3, the crosshatching is still soft, which is attributed to the Sharpness value being only 2. Compare this to the image on the opposite page that also uses the highest Strength.

ORIGINAL IMAGE

Settings
Stroke Length 5
Sharpness 20
Strength 1

Settings
Stroke Length 20
Sharpness 2
Strength 3

INTRODUCING DARK STROKES

This filter name is something of a misnomer since the filter draws strokes over both dark and light areas of an image. Increasing the Balance setting determines whether the midtones are affected, while the Black and White Intensity levels increasingly turn the image into strong black and white areas.

ORIGINAL IMAGE

DEFAULT DARK STROKES
The Default settings create an effect where the dark strokes overwhelm the main subject of the image.

Settings
Balance 5
Black Intensity 6
White Intensity 2

ADJUSTING BLACK INTENSITY
Taking the Default settings and simply adjusting the Black Intensity gives a much lighter result.

Settings
Balance 5
Black Intensity 1
White Intensity 2

DEFAULT

Dark Strok

Balance

Black Inte

White Inte

DEFAULT

Dark Strokes

Balance	5
Black Intensity	6
White Intensity	2

FILTER SETTING PARAMETERS

Balance	Min **0**	Max **10**
Black Intensity	Min **0**	Max **10**
White Intensity	Min **0**	Max **10**

BLACK
INTENSITY

STROKES IN ALL TONAL LEVELS

Increasing the Balance value creates strokes in the midtones, as you can see in the trees.

Settings
Balance 10
Black Intensity 1
White Intensity 2

ORIGINAL IMAGE

BRIGHT WHITES

The White Intensity has been maximized at the same time as having the high Balance setting and a reasonable Black Intensity to create this strong graphic image.

Settings
Balance 10
Black Intensity 4
White Intensity 10

BRIGHTENING

White Intensity intensifies the flowers and the green leaves, which look fluorescent.

Settings
Balance 2
Black Intensity 0
White Intensity 10

Balance
Black I
White

ORIGINAL IMAGE

USING BLACK INTENSITY

With the same value for Black Intensity as in the Default image on the opposite spread, here the effect is to create a moodiness, with the pink/white flowers standing out against the black.

Settings
Balance 8
Black Intensity 6
White Intensity 2

INTRODUCING INK OUTLINES

This filter draws white and black outlines around the edges featured in an image. The settings offer adjustments to the Stroke Length, which offsets the line and strengthens the highlights as its value is increased. The Dark and Light Intensity change the shadows and highlights, respectively.

ORIGINAL IMAGE

DEFAULT INK OUTLINES
The Ink Outlines filter works well on an image with lots of detail, both highlighting the lines in this building and outlining the clouds.

Settings
Stroke Length 4
Dark Intensity 20
Light Intensity 10

DELICATE LINES
Just changing the Stroke Length to its maximum setting gives a blurred, more delicate effect.

Settings
Stroke Length 50
Dark Intensity 20
Light Intensity 10

DEFAULT

Ink Outlines

Stroke Length   4

Dark Intensity   20

Light Intensity   10

FILTER SETTING PARAMETERS

Stroke Length	Min **1**	Max **50**
Dark Intensity	Min **0**	Max **50**
Light Intensity	Min **0**	Max **50**

ALL DETAIL OUTLINED
The Dark Intensity displays the myriad of lines in these oranges with a highlighted detail.

Settings
Stroke Length 1
Dark Intensity 30
Light Intensity 10

ORIGINAL IMAGE

LIGHTER EFFECT
Reducing the Dark Intensity to 0 brightens the whole image and causes the ink outlines to recede.

Settings
Stroke Length 25
Dark Intensity 0
Light Intensity 10

ORIGINAL IMAGE

SHARP OUTLINES
Increasing both the Dark and Light Intensity to 30, while keeping the Stroke Length short, creates this sharpened effect with the outlines.

Settings
Stroke Length 1
Dark Intensity 30
Light Intensity 30

INTENSE OUTLINES
The intense color shifts around the baskets appear when the Light Intensity is almost at maximum.

Settings
Stroke Length 8
Dark Intensity 10
Light Intensity 40

FILTER GALLERY

INK OUTLINES

DEFAULT

STROKE LENGTH

Stroke Length 15
Dark Intensity 20
Light Intensity 10

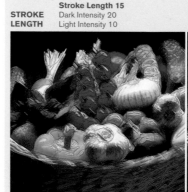

Stroke Length 35
Dark Intensity 20
Light Intensity 10

Stroke Length 4
Dark Intensity 50
Light Intensity 10

LIGHT INTENSITY

Stroke Length 4
Dark Intensity 20
Light Intensity 0

Stroke Length 4
Dark Intensity 20
Light Intensity 20

Stroke Length 25
Dark Intensity 30
Light Intensity 50

Stroke Length 50
Dark Intensity 10
Light Intensity 0

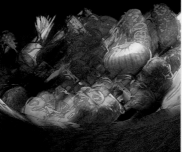

Stroke Length 12
Dark Intensity 50
Light Intensity 10

DEFAULT

Ink Outlines

Stroke Length **4**

Dark Intensity **20**

Light Intensity **10**

FILTER SETTING PARAMETERS

Stroke Length	Min **1**	Max **50**
Dark Intensity	Min **0**	Max **50**
Light Intensity	Min **0**	Max **50**

Stroke Length 50
Dark Intensity 20
Light Intensity 10

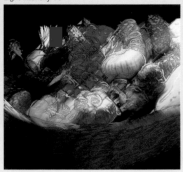

DARK INTENSITY
Stroke Length 4
Dark Intensity 0
Light Intensity 10

Stroke Length 4
Dark Intensity 35
Light Intensity 10

Stroke Length 4
Dark Intensity 20
Light Intensity 35

Stroke Length 4
Dark Intensity 20
Light Intensity 50

MIXED SETTINGS
Stroke Length 1
Dark Intensity 0
Light Intensity 50

Stroke Length 15
Dark Intensity 5
Light Intensity 50

Stroke Length 30
Dark Intensity 10
Light Intensity 10

Stroke Length 50
Dark Intensity 50
Light Intensity 50

INTRODUCING SPATTER

Designed to imitate painting with an airbrush, the Spatter filter creates a lightly rippled effect to your image. How far the spatter spreads is determined by the value of the Spray Radius setting. The Smoothness setting softens the spatter, making it less jagged.

ORIGINAL IMAGE

DEFAULT SPATTER
The spattering distorts the edges, but, with the default settings, the image is still discernible.

Settings
Spray Radius 10
Smoothness 5

LARGER SPRAY
With Spray Radius and Smoothness set to maximum and minimum, respectively, an unintelligible but colorful abstract is the result.

Settings
Spray Radius 25
Smoothness 1

DEFAULT

Spatter	⇕
Spray Radius	10
Smoothness	5

FILTER SETTING PARAMETERS

Spray Radius	Min **0**	Max **25**
Smoothness	Min **1**	Max **15**

FINE SPATTER
Here Spray Radius has been reduced to 3 and Smoothness is only 1, creating a very fine effect.

Settings
Spray Radius 3
Smoothness 1

ORIGINAL IMAGE

SUBTLE SPRAY
Right: The spatter here is fairly minimal, gently distorting the edges.

Settings
Spray Radius 6
Smoothness 5

ORIGINAL IMAGE

SPATTERING THE EDGES
In both of the images to the left, Spatter distorts the edges to a much greater degree due to Spray Radius being high. In the right-hand image, it's at its maximum.

Settings
Spray Radius 20
Smoothness 7

Settings
Spray Radius 25
Smoothness 7

SPATTER

DEFAULT

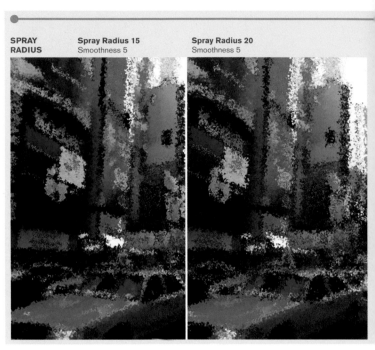

SPRAY RADIUS

Spray Radius 15
Smoothness 5

Spray Radius 20
Smoothness 5

Spray Radius 10
Smoothness 10

MIXED SETTINGS

Spray Radius 20
Smoothness 10

Spray Radius 5
Smoothness 1

DEFAULT

FILTER SETTING PARAMETERS

Spray Radius	Min **0**	Max **25**
Smoothness	Min **1**	Max **15**

Spray Radius 25
Smoothness 5

SMOOTHNESS   Spray Radius 10
                        Smoothness 1

Spray Radius 10
Smoothness 3

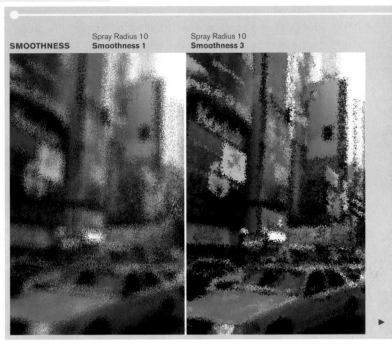

Spray Radius 25
Smoothness 1

Spray Radius 6
Smoothness 3

Spray Radius 25
Smoothness 10

INTRODUCING SPRAYED STROKES

This filter is at its strongest when applied to images with areas of contrasting color and definite edges, since the effect is mainly applied to edges. As well as being able to control the Stroke Length, you can also adjust the Spray Radius to determine how far the spray spreads. Changing the Stroke Direction can make a significant difference to the impact of the filter.

ORIGINAL IMAGE

DEFAULT SPRAYED STROKES
The filter puts a shimmer over this image when the default settings are applied.

Settings
Stroke Length 12
Spray Radius 7
Stroke Direction: Right Diagonal

TURNING THE SPRAYED STROKES
Here Stroke Direction has been changed to Left Diagonal and Spray Radius has been increased, spreading the spray effect.

Settings
Stroke Length 12
Spray Radius 16
Stroke Direction: Left Diagonal

DEFAULT

Sprayed Strokes	
Stroke Length	12
Spray Radius	7
Stroke Direction:	Right Diagonal

FILTER SETTING PARAMETERS

Stroke Length	Min **0**	Max **20**
Spray Radius	Min **0**	Max **25**

MOTTLED EFFECT

Reducing Stroke Length to 0 while keeping Spray Radius low creates this mottled effect.

Settings
Stroke Length 0
Spray Radius 2
Stroke Direction:
Right Diagonal

ORIGINAL IMAGE

MORE GRANULATION

Increasing Spray Radius to 7 makes the image even more blotchy.

Settings
Stroke Length 0
Spray Radius 7
Stroke Direction: Right Diagonal

ORIGINAL IMAGE

TEXTURED EFFECTS

Increasing both Stroke Length and Spray Radius gives a longer sprayed stroke. In the image to the far right, Stroke Length and Stroke Radius are at maximum and Stroke Direction has changed to Vertical.

Settings
Stroke Length 20
Spray Radius 10
Stroke Direction: Right Diagonal

Settings
Stroke Length 20
Spray Radius 25
Stroke Direction: Vertical

SPRAYED STROKES

DEFAULT

STROKE LENGTH

Stroke Length 0
Spray Radius 7
Stroke Direction: Right Diagonal

Stroke Length 6
Spray Radius 7
Stroke Direction: Right Diagonal

Stroke Length 12
Spray Radius 19
Stroke Direction: Right Diagonal

Stroke Length 12
Spray Radius 25
Stroke Direction: Right Diagonal

STROKE DIRECTION

Stroke Length 12
Spray Radius 7
Stroke Direction: Horizontal

DEFAULT

Sprayed Strokes

Stroke Length 12

Spray Radius 7

Stroke Direction: Right Diagonal

FILTER SETTING PARAMETERS

Stroke Length	Min **0**	Max **20**
Spray Radius	Min **0**	Max **25**

Stroke Length 20
Spray Radius 7
Stroke Direction: Right Diagonal

SPRAY RADIUS

Stroke Length 12
Spray Radius 2
Stroke Direction: Right Diagonal

Stroke Length 12
Spray Radius 13
Stroke Direction: Right Diagonal

Stroke Length 12
Spray Radius 7
Stroke Direction: Left Diagonal

Stroke Length 12
Spray Radius 7
Stroke Direction: Vertical

MIXED SETTINGS

Stroke Length 3
Spray Radius 6
Stroke Direction: Left Diagonal

INTRODUCING SUMI-E

Designed to mimic the Japanese art of painting with black ink, the Sumi-e filter adds dark strokes to areas of color. The width of the strokes are determined by Stroke Width, while Stroke Pressure increases the prominence of the smaller strokes. You can also vary the overall contrast of the whole image by moving the Contrast slider.

ORIGINAL IMAGE

DEFAULT SUMI-E
The thick black lines and the moderately high contrast of the default setting create a wash with thick, dark outlines.

Settings
Stroke Width 10
Stroke Pressure 2
Contrast 16

LIGHTENED STROKES
Reducing only
Stroke Width lightens
the whole image.

Settings
Stroke Width 3
Stroke Pressure 2
Contrast 16

DEFAULT

Sumi-e	
Stroke Width	10
Stroke Pressure	2
Contrast	16

FILTER SETTING PARAMETERS

Stroke Width	Min **3**	Max **15**
Stroke Pressure	Min **0**	Max **15**
Contrast	Min **0**	Max **40**

FINE LINES
Low Stroke Width, Stroke Pressure, and Contrast give this finer-lined effect.

Settings
Stroke Width 5
Stroke Pressure 3
Contrast 0

ORIGINAL IMAGE

HEAVIER LINES
Without increasing Contrast, the lines have been thickened by increasing Stroke Width and Stroke Pressure.

Settings
Stroke Width 10
Stroke Pressure 8
Contrast 0

ORIGINAL IMAGE

DELICATE MARKS
With Stroke Pressure set higher than Stroke Width, much of the detail in the image is delicately pulled out.

Settings
Stroke Width 3
Stroke Pressure 15
Contrast 6

Settings
Stroke Width 11
Stroke Pressure 7
Contrast 6

DEFINITE OUTLINES
Stroke Width has been increased, giving more definite outlines, while many of the details have receded due to reduced Stroke Pressure.

SUMI-E

DEFAULT

| STROKE WIDTH | **Stroke Width 3** Stroke Pressure 2 Contrast 16 | **Stroke Width 15** Stroke Pressure 2 Contrast 16 |

Stroke Width 10
Stroke Pressure 2
Contrast 40

| MIXED SETTINGS | **Stroke Width 3** **Stroke Pressure 15** Contrast 16 | **Stroke Width 15** **Stroke Pressure 10** **Contrast 0** |

DEFAULT

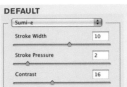

| Sumi–e | | |

Stroke Width 10

Stroke Pressure 2

Contrast 16

FILTER SETTING PARAMETERS

Stroke Width	Min 3	Max 15
Stroke Pressure	Min 0	Max 15
Contrast	Min 0	Max 40

STROKE PRESSURE

Stroke Width 10
Stroke Pressure 0
Contrast 16

Stroke Width 10
Stroke Pressure 15
Contrast 16

CONTRAST

Stroke Width 10
Stroke Pressure 2
Contrast 0

Stroke Width 5
Stroke Pressure 0
Contrast 25

Stroke Width 10
Stroke Pressure 8
Contrast 5

Stroke Width 5
Stroke Pressure 5
Contrast 20

DISTORT FILTERS

Only three of the twelve Distort filters are available through Photoshop's Filter Gallery—Diffuse Glow, Glass, and Ocean Ripple. The rest of the filters are covered in the Other Filter Effects section on pages 350–367. The Distort filters, as you would expect, distort your image, sometimes to the point where you're left with a picture that is unrecognizable from its original. However, there are also plenty more subtle results, as you'll see in the pages that follow.

INTRODUCING DIFFUSE GLOW

The Diffuse Glow filter adds a soft glow to the image using the background color. It focuses the glow on the background of the image, making the photograph look as though it were shot through a diffuse filter. The Graininess setting adds noise, while the Glow Amount controls how bright the glow is, and the Clear Amount determines how much of the image is covered by the glow.

ORIGINAL IMAGE

DEFAULT DIFFUSE GLOW
The default setting was applied with a default white Background Color. The glow is added to the toadstools, leaving the grass largely unaffected.

Settings
Graininess 6
Glow Amount 10
Clear Amount 15

Foreground/
Background Colors

WHITE HIGHLIGHTS
With minimum Graininess, but a high Glow Amount, the toadstools have a very bright, clear glow. More of the grass is affected due to the lower Clear Amount setting.

Settings
Graininess 1
Glow Amount 15
Clear Amount 7

DEFAULT

Diffuse Glow

Graininess	6
Glow Amount	10
Clear Amount	15

FILTER SETTING PARAMETERS

Graininess	Min **0**	Max **10**
Glow Amount	Min **0**	Max **20**
Clear Amount	Min **0**	Max **20**

FOGGY EFFECT

By reducing the Clear Amount, the glow covers most of the image. Keeping the Graininess reasonably low gives the impression of mist over the water.

Settings
Graininess 3
Glow Amount 8
Clear Amount 3

ORIGINAL IMAGE

GRAINY EFFECT

With a high setting for both Glow Amount and Clear Amount, the glow is focused around the back of the gondolas, blurring the buildings in the background.

Settings
Graininess 10
Glow Amount 14
Clear Amount 20

KNOCKING BACK

Here the glow provides a means to knock back the image, creating an interesting textured effect with a high Graininess setting.

Settings
Graininess 10
Glow Amount 9
Clear Amount 4

ORIGINAL IMAGE

CREATING ATMOSPHERE

Using the Clear Amount setting to limit the glow to the background, the foreground trees stand out, with an atmospheric mist behind them.

Settings
Graininess 0
Glow Amount 4
Clear Amount 12

INTRODUCING GLASS

If you need to give the impression of looking at an image through glass, this filter will help you achieve it. Offering a selection of different glass-like textures, the prominence of the pattern can be controlled by adjusting Distortion; the focus by moving the Smoothness slider. You can also scale the Texture, as with other Photoshop filters.

ORIGINAL IMAGE

DEFAULT GLASS
When applied with the Default settings, it seems as though the image is being viewed through frosted glass.

Settings
Distortion 5
Smoothness 3
Texture: Frosted
Scaling 100%

LESS DISTORTION
The higher the Smoothness setting, the more the distortion is minimized, so that in this image, a gentle pattern enhances the detail.

Settings
Distortion 15
Smoothness 10
Texture: Frosted
Scaling 100%

DEFAULT

Glass	
Distortion	5
Smoothness	3
Texture:	Frosted
Scaling	100 %

FILTER SETTING PARAMETERS

Distortion	Min **0**	Max **20**
Smoothness	Min **1**	Max **15**

ORIGINAL IMAGE

FINE DISTORTION
Below: Reducing the Distortion value reduces the size of the glass pattern, so that it appears as a finer distortion.

Settings
Distortion 2
Smoothness 3
Texture: Frosted
Scaling 100%

BLOCK DISTORTION
Changing the Texture to Blocks divides up the image, giving each block its own distortion and making the building look like one designed by Gaudi.

Settings
Distortion 7
Smoothness 15
Texture: Blocks
Scaling 100%

USING DIFFERENT TEXTURES
Adjusting both the Texture type and its Scaling offers a myriad of results and could be used to lose all detail in an image, providing instead an interesting background texture.

ORIGINAL IMAGE

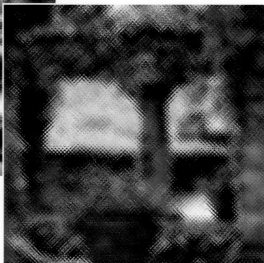

Settings
Distortion 1
Smoothness 1
Texture: Canvas
Scaling 200%

Settings
Distortion 12
Smoothness 5
Texture: Tiny Lens
Scaling 50%

GLASS

DEFAULT

DISTORTION

Distortion 1
Smoothness 3
Texture: Frosted; Scaling 100%

Distortion 10
Smoothness 3
Texture: Frosted; Scaling 100%

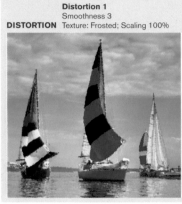

Distortion 5
Smoothness 8
Texture: Frosted; Scaling 100%

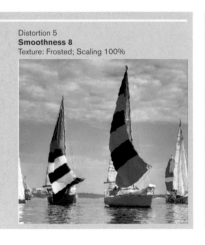

TEXTURE

Distortion 5
Smoothness 3
Texture: Blocks; Scaling 100%

Distortion 5
Smoothness 3
Texture: Canvas; Scaling 100%

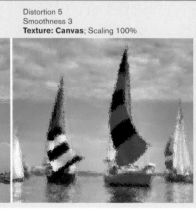

MIXED SETTINGS

Distortion 10
Smoothness 7
Texture: Frosted; Scaling 100%

Distortion 20
Smoothness 15
Texture: Frosted; Scaling 100%

Distortion 16
Smoothness 1
Texture: Canvas; Scaling 100%

DEFAULT

Glass

Distortion	5
Smoothness	3
Texture:	Frosted
Scaling	100 %

FILTER SETTING PARAMETERS

Distortion	Min **0**	Max **20**
Smoothness	Min **1**	Max **15**

Distortion 20
Smoothness 3
Texture: Frosted; Scaling 100%

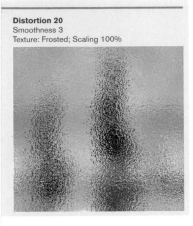

SMOOTHNESS

Distortion 5
Smoothness 1
Texture: Frosted; Scaling 100%

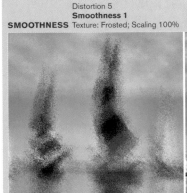

Distortion 5
Smoothness 6
Texture: Frosted; Scaling 100%

Distortion 5
Smoothness 3
Texture: Tiny Lens; Scaling 100%

SCALING

Distortion 5
Smoothness 3
Texture: Frosted; **Scaling 50%**

Distortion 5
Smoothness 3
Texture: Frosted; **Scaling 200%**

Distortion 6
Smoothness 4
Texture: Canvas; Scaling 50%

Distortion 4
Smoothness 9
Texture: Blocks; Scaling 54%

Distortion 1
Smoothness 1
Texture: Frosted; **Scaling 50%**

SKETCH FILTERS

Many of the Sketch filters produce a two-tone effect, taking the coloring from the Foreground and Background Colors. All 14 filters are available through the Filter Gallery, and many require their settings to be played with if you want to be left with a recognizable image. This section shows you clearly how the settings you choose vary the effect of the filter.

INTRODUCING BAS RELIEF

The Bas Relief filter creates a sculpted impression of the image using the Foreground and Background Colors. The Foreground Color replaces the shadow areas, and the Background Color highlights areas in the image, which means that using the default colors creates a grayscale image, but you can change the colors. Adjusting the Light direction can make the image look as though it is either raised from the paper or indented.

ORIGINAL IMAGE

DEFAULT BAS RELIEF
The default settings give the impression that the picture has been molded from a sheet of metal.

Foreground/
Background
Colors

Settings
Detail 13
Smoothness 3
Light: Bottom

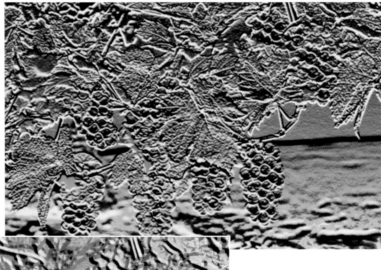

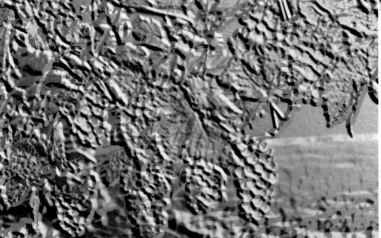

OPPOSITE LIGHT DIRECTION
The same image looks different here, mainly because the Light direction is coming from the Top Right. There is less detail, which knocks the image out of focus.

Settings
Detail 9
Smoothness 1
Light: Top Right

DEFAULT

Bas Relief
Detail 13
Smoothness 3
Light: Bottom

FILTER SETTING PARAMETERS

Detail	Min **1**	Max **15**
Smoothness	Min **1**	Max **15**

MAXIMUM DETAIL
This application of the filter uses the maximum amount of Detail and minimum Smoothness, giving sharp edges.

Settings
Detail 15
Smoothness 1
Light: Bottom Right

ORIGINAL IMAGE

Settings
Detail 15
Smoothness 1
Light: Right

Foreground/
Background Colors

BRASS SHEETING
The Foreground and Background Colors have been changed and combined with the high level of Detail and minimal Smoothness, creating the impression of imprinted brass sheeting.

ORIGINAL IMAGE

CONTOUR EFFECTS
Using lower values for Detail and Smoothness, these two images have a relief that follows the general contours of the feathers. Notice also the way the graduated background has been translated.

Settings
Detail 10
Smoothness 1
Light: Bottom Right

Settings
Detail 7
Smoothness 4
Light: Left

Foreground/
Background Colors

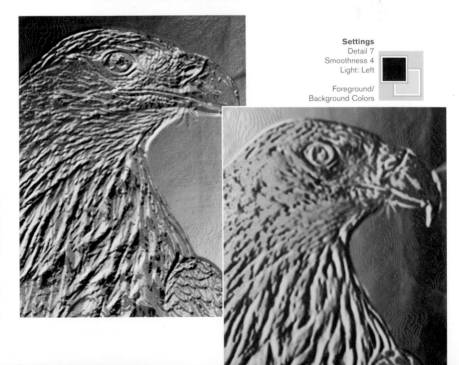

BAS RELIEF

DEFAULT

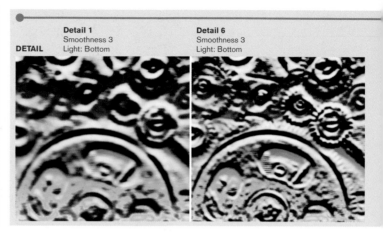

DETAIL

Detail 1
Smoothness 3
Light: Bottom

Detail 6
Smoothness 3
Light: Bottom

Detail 13
Smoothness 10
Light: Bottom

Detail 13
Smoothness 15
Light: Bottom

LIGHT

Detail 13
Smoothness 3
Light: Bottom Left

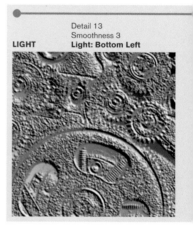

Detail 13
Smoothness 3
Light: Top Right

Detail 13
Smoothness 3
Light: Right

Detail 13
Smoothness 3
Light: Bottom Right

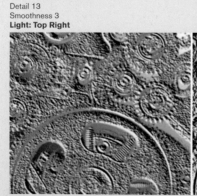

DEFAULT

FILTER SETTING PARAMETERS

Detail	Min	1	Max	15
Smoothness	Min	1	Max	15

Detail 15
Smoothness 3
Light: Bottom

SMOOTHNESS

Detail 13
Smoothness 1
Light: Bottom

Detail 13
Smoothness 6
Light: Bottom

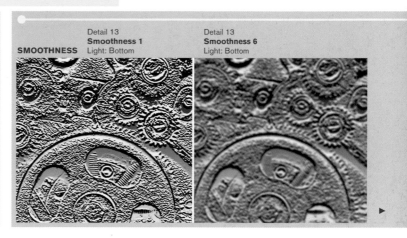

Detail 13
Smoothness 3
Light: Left

Detail 13
Smoothness 3
Light: Top Left

Detail 13
Smoothness 3
Light: Top

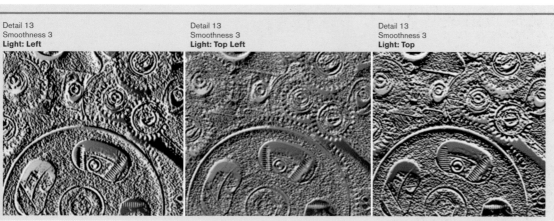

**MIXED
SETTINGS**

Detail 2
Smoothness 1
Light: Right

Detail 15
Smoothness 1
Light: Top Left

Detail 10
Smoothness 15
Light: Left

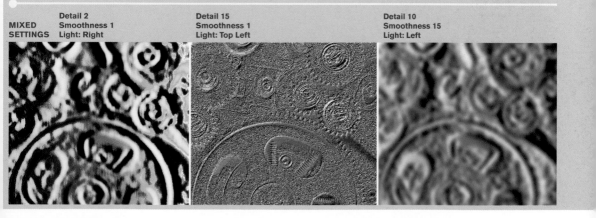

INTRODUCING CHALK & CHARCOAL

When this filter is applied, it tries to replicate an image drawn in chalk and charcoal. It does this by creating diagonal strokes: in the Foreground Color for the shadows to mimic the charcoal, and in the opposite direction in the Background Color for the highlights and midtones to mimic the chalk. It means that you don't have to work in black and white, but to mimic chalk you need to ensure that your Background Color is lighter than your Foreground Color.

ORIGINAL IMAGE

Foreground/
Background
Colors

DEFAULT CHALK & CHARCOAL
Using the default filter settings with a black Foreground Color and white Background Color creates a chalky grayscale sketch.

Settings
Charcoal Area 6
Chalk Area 6
Stroke Pressure 1

THICK STROKES
The Foreground and Background Colors have been changed to yellow and blue, and there are much heavier, thicker charcoal strokes, which cover the shadow areas. Most of the areas that would have been covered with chalk strokes are gray.

Settings
Charcoal Area 15
Chalk Area 0
Stroke Pressure 3

Foreground/
Background Colors

DEFAULT

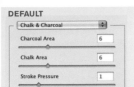

Chalk & Charcoal	
Charcoal Area	6
Chalk Area	6
Stroke Pressure	1

FILTER SETTING PARAMETERS

	Min	Max
Charcoal Area	0	20
Chalk Area	0	20
Stroke Pressure	0	5

CHALK DOMINATING

The Chalk Area is prominent here, resulting in a much lighter image, with the charcoal less apparent.

Settings
Charcoal Area 1
Chalk Area 20
Stroke Pressure 2

ORIGINAL IMAGE

COLORED CHARCOAL

By changing the Foreground Color, the charcoal color changes. These settings use equal amounts of Charcoal Area and Chalk Area with a low Stroke Pressure.

Settings
Charcoal Area 10
Chalk Area 10
Stroke Pressure 1

Foreground/Background Colors

Settings
Charcoal Area 9
Chalk Area 0
Stroke Pressure 1

ORIGINAL IMAGE

SKETCH EFFECTS

Both of these images are aiming for a more traditional sketch effect. The right-hand image shows a rougher texture as the filter has been applied twice.

Settings
Charcoal Area 9
Chalk Area 0
Stroke Pressure 1

CHALK & CHARCOAL

DEFAULT

**CHARCOAL
AREA**

Charcoal Area 0
Chalk Area 6
Stroke Pressure 1

Charcoal Area 13
Chalk Area 6
Stroke Pressure 1

Charcoal Area 6
Chalk Area 6
Stroke Pressure 5

**MIXED
SETTINGS**

Charcoal Area 20
Chalk Area 20
Stroke Pressure 1

Charcoal Area 10
Chalk Area 12
Stroke Pressure 1

DEFAULT

FILTER SETTING PARAMETERS

Charcoal Area	Min **0**	Max **20**
Chalk Area	Min **0**	Max **20**
Stroke Pressure	Min **0**	Max **5**

Charcoal Area 20
Chalk Area 6
Stroke Pressure 1

CHALK AREA Charcoal Area 6
Chalk Area 20
Stroke Pressure 1

STROKE PRESSURE Charcoal Area 6
Chalk Area 6
Stroke Pressure 0

Charcoal Area 0
Chalk Area 20
Stroke Pressure 3

Charcoal Area 20
Chalk Area 5
Stroke Pressure 3

Charcoal Area 5
Chalk Area 15
Stroke Pressure 2

INTRODUCING CHARCOAL

This is a simpler filter than Chalk & Charcoal (see pages 178–181) that uses the Foreground Color to apply charcoal around the strongest edges of an image. The Background Color is the "paper" color. The settings allow you to control how thick the strokes are (Charcoal Thickness), how much detail there is, and how much weight is given to the strokes.

ORIGINAL IMAGE

Foreground/
Background
Colors

DEFAULT CHARCOAL
Although this effect doesn't resemble a charcoal sketch, it nonetheless provides a delicately pleasing result.

Settings
Charcoal Thickness 1
Detail 5
Light/Dark Balance 50

**DARKENING
THE IMAGE**
The only setting that has changed here is the Light/Dark Balance, which makes the charcoal appear more heavily applied.

Settings
Charcoal Thickness 1
Detail 5
Light/Dark Balance 90

DEFAULT

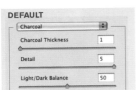

Charcoal	
Charcoal Thickness	1
Detail	5
Light/Dark Balance	50

FILTER SETTING PARAMETERS

Charcoal Thickness Min **1**	Max **7**
Detail Min **0**	Max **5**
Light/Dark Balance Min **0**	Max **100**

MORE CHARCOAL

Increasing Charcoal Thickness creates more areas of charcoal, so that more of the background is filled with strokes than would be with a lower value.

Settings
Charcoal Thickness 3
Detail 3
Light/Dark Balance 70

ORIGINAL IMAGE

THICKER CHARCOAL

Charcoal Thickness is at its maximum while Detail is at its minimum, giving the effect of thick charcoal strokes over the most prominent edges.

Settings
Charcoal Thickness 7
Detail 0
Light/Dark Balance 80

LESS DETAIL

Minimizing Charcoal Thickness and Detail while increasing the Light/Dark Balance results in this image that has the look of smudged charcoal.

CHANGING COLORS

Changing the Background Color gives a different paper color, and, although charcoal in real life can only be black or gray, it has a green tinge to it here, having changed the Foreground Color.

ORIGINAL IMAGE

Settings
Charcoal Thickness 4
Detail 5
Light/Dark Balance 40

Foreground/
Background Colors

Settings
Charcoal Thickness 1
Detail 0
Light/Dark Balance 80

INTRODUCING CHROME

This is one of the most widely used Photoshop filters. It gives a metallic look to an image, as though it has been molded out of shiny metal. The Detail and Smoothness settings generally work better on photographs that have definite and strong shapes. Unlike most other Sketch filters, changing the Foreground and Background Colors has no effect on the Chrome filter.

ORIGINAL IMAGE

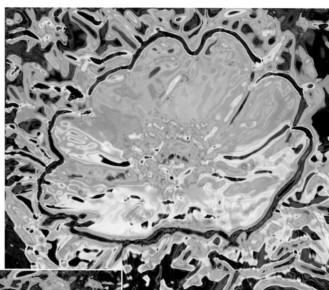

DEFAULT CHROME
With many images, the original shapes disintegrate when the filter is applied. With this large, bold image of the flower, the shape is retained in the chrome effect.

Settings
Detail 4
Smoothness 7

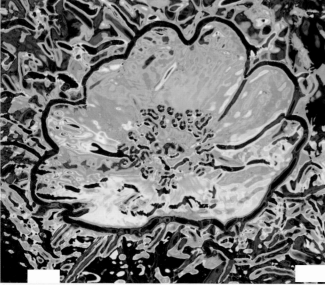

SHARPENING DETAIL
Reducing the Smoothness to 0 gives more detail to the image, with the edges more clearly defined in dark gray.

Settings
Detail 4
Smoothness 0

DEFAULT

Chrome	
Detail	4
Smoothness	7

FILTER SETTING PARAMETERS

Detail	Min **0**	Max **10**
Smoothness	Min **0**	Max **10**

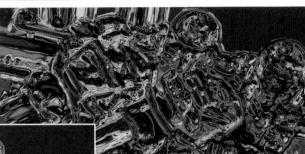

ORIGINAL IMAGE

TEXTURE
Using a high level of Detail and Smoothness means the shapes in this image are barely decipherable, but the texture is enhanced.

Settings
Detail 8
Smoothness 10

METALLIC EFFECT
Using the lowest Detail value and the highest Smoothness value creates a smoother result.

Settings
Detail 0
Smoothness 10

ROUNDED EDGES
Tweaking the amount of Detail and Smoothness gives rounded edges to the image.

Settings
Detail 7
Smoothness 2

ORIGINAL IMAGE

MOLDED CHROME
Using the highest value for Detail and the lowest for Smoothness can give a sense of crinkled aluminum foil.

Settings
Detail 10
Smoothness 0

CHROME

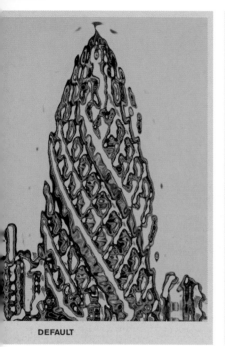

DEFAULT

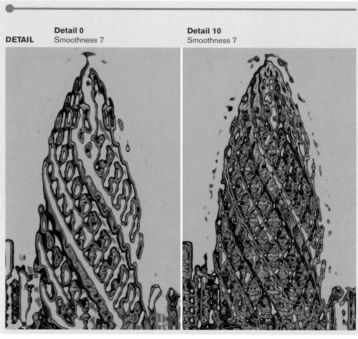

DETAIL

Detail 0
Smoothness 7

Detail 10
Smoothness 7

Detail 10
Smoothness 2

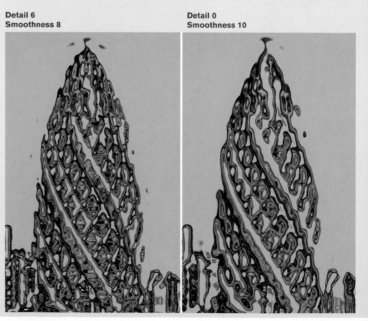

Detail 6
Smoothness 8

Detail 0
Smoothness 10

DEFAULT

Chrome

Detail   4

Smoothness   7

FILTER SETTING PARAMETERS

| Detail | Min **0** | Max **10** |
| Smoothness | Min **0** | Max **10** |

SMOOTHNESS   Detail 4
Smoothness 0

Detail 4
Smoothness 10

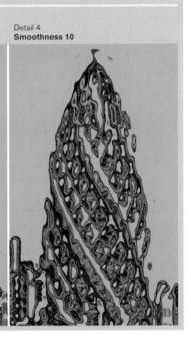

**MIXED
SETTINGS**   Detail 1
Smoothness 1

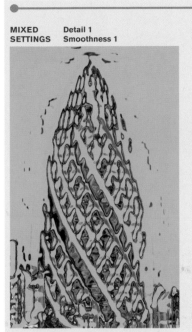

Detail 10
Smoothness 6

Detail 8
Smoothness 1

Detail 0
Smoothness 5

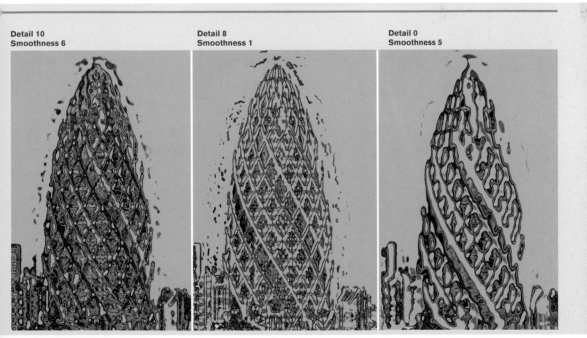

INTRODUCING CONTÉ CRAYON

Using the Foreground and Background Colors to create two-colored strokes on a textured background, this filter produces a similar effect to the Rough Pastels filter (see pages 76–93). You can adjust the Foreground and Background Levels to control how the highlights and shadows in the image are translated into strokes using either the Foreground or the Background Color.

ORIGINAL IMAGE

Foreground/
Background
Colors

**DEFAULT CONTÉ
CRAYON**
Using the default Foreground and Background Colors creates highlights in white, shadows in black, and midtones in gray.

Settings
Foreground Level 11
Background Level 7
Texture: Canvas
Scaling 100%
Relief 4
Light: Top

USING COLOR
Taking colors from the image for the Foreground and Background Colors gives a tinted effect with gray still covering the midtones, although the higher Foreground and Background Levels reduce the amount of gray.

Settings
Foreground Level 14
Background Level 11
Texture: Canvas
Scaling 100%
Relief 4
Light: Top

Foreground/
Background Colors

DEFAULT

FILTER SETTING PARAMETERS

Foreground Level Min **1**   Max **15**

Background Level Min **1**   Max **15**

LIGHTER SHADES

With a higher Background Level value, there is more emphasis on the highlights and less on the shadows. This image also uses a Sandstone Texture.

Settings
Foreground Level 5
Background Level 12
Texture: Sandstone
Scaling 50%
Relief 10
Light: Top

ORIGINAL IMAGE

Foreground/
Background Colors

STRONGER CONTRAST

Using both high Foreground and Background Level settings produces this strongly contrasted effect. The image also uses a Burlap Texture, with a low level of Relief.

Settings
Foreground Level 13
Background Level 10
Texture: Burlap
Scaling 125%
Relief 2
Light: Bottom Left

ORIGINAL IMAGE

STRONG TEXTURE

This image uses a prominent Burlap Texture with grays, and Foreground and Background Colors taken from the original image.

Settings
Foreground Level 12
Background Level 9
Texture: Burlap
Scaling 115%
Relief 3
Light: Top

Foreground/
Background
Colors

LESS GRAY

As the Foreground and Background Levels increase, the amount of gray is reduced. The image also uses a Sandstone Texture with high relief.

Settings
Foreground Level 13
Background Level 15
Texture: Sandstone
Scaling 75%
Relief 5
Light: Top

CONTÉ CRAYON
CANVAS

DEFAULT CANVAS TEXTURE

FOREGROUND LEVEL

Foreground Level 1
Background Level 7

BACKGROUND LEVEL

Foreground Level 11
Background Level 1

Foreground Level 11
Background Level 5

MIXED SETTINGS

Foreground Level 8
Background Level 8

Foreground Level 1
Background Level 15

DEFAULT

Conté Crayon

Foreground Level   11

Background Level   7

Texture: Canvas

FILTER SETTING PARAMETERS

Foreground Level   Min **1**   Max **15**

Background Level   Min **1**   Max **15**

These images show the default Canvas Texture with variations in the Foreground Level and Background Level settings. See pages 194–195 for variations in Texture settings.

Foreground Level 6
Background Level 7

Foreground Level 13
Background Level 7

Foreground Level 11
Background Level 12

Foreground Level 11
Background Level 15

Foreground Level 15
Background Level 8

Foreground Level 4
Background Level 11

CONTÉ CRAYON
CANVAS (CONTINUED)

TEXTURE SETTINGS

Scaling 50%
Relief 4
Light: Top

Scaling 150%
Relief 4
Light: Top

MIXED SETTINGS

Foreground Level 11
Background Level 7

Scaling 50%
Relief 10
Light: Top

Foreground Level 5
Background Level 15

Scaling 50%
Relief 30
Light: Top

CANVAS TEXTURE SETTINGS

DEFAULT

Texture:	Canvas
Scaling	100 %
Relief	4
Light:	Top

FILTER SETTING PARAMETERS

Scaling	Min **50%**	Max **200%**
Relief	Min **0**	Max **50**

These images show variations in the Scaling and Relief Texture settings, and mixed settings of all options.

Scaling 100%
Relief 1
Light: Top

Scaling 100%
Relief 10
Light: Top

Foreground Level 5
Background Level 5

Scaling 200%
Relief 2
Light: Top

Foreground Level 15
Background Level 15

Scaling 115%
Relief 20
Light: Top

CONTÉ CRAYON
BRICK

DEFAULT BRICK TEXTURE

FOREGROUND LEVEL — **Foreground Level 1**
Background Level 7

BACKGROUND LEVEL — Foreground Level 11
Background Level 1

Foreground Level 11
Background Level 5

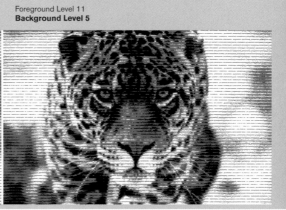

MIXED SETTINGS — **Foreground Level 8**
Background Level 8

Foreground Level 1
Background Level 15

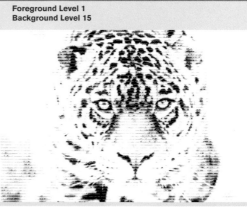

DEFAULT

Conté Crayon

Foreground Level 11

Background Level 7

Texture: Brick

FILTER SETTING PARAMETERS

Foreground Level   Min **1**   Max **15**

Background Level   Min **1**   Max **15**

These images show Brick Texture with variations in the Foreground Level and Background Level settings. See pages 198–199 for variations in Texture settings.

Foreground Level 6
Background Level 7

Foreground Level 13
Background Level 7

Foreground Level 11
Background Level 12

Foreground Level 11
Background Level 15

Foreground Level 15
Background Level 8

Foreground Level 4
Background Level 11

CONTÉ CRAYON
BURLAP

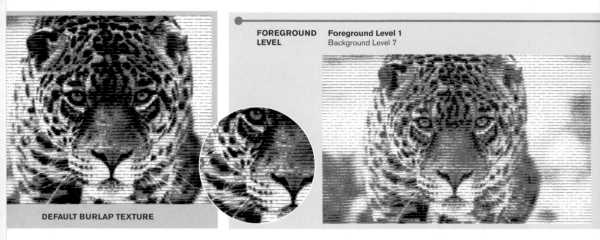

DEFAULT BURLAP TEXTURE

FOREGROUND LEVEL — **Foreground Level 1** / Background Level 7

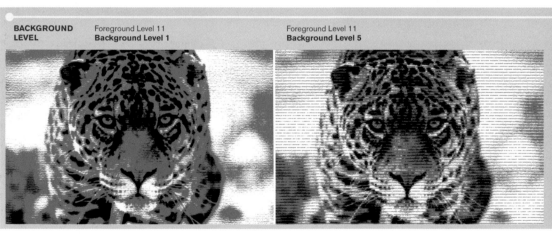

BACKGROUND LEVEL — Foreground Level 11 / **Background Level 1**

Foreground Level 11 / **Background Level 5**

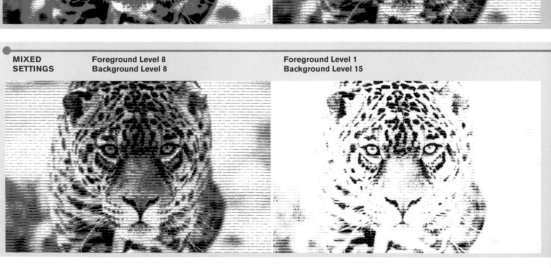

MIXED SETTINGS — **Foreground Level 8** / **Background Level 8**

Foreground Level 1 / **Background Level 15**

DEFAULT

Conté Crayon

Foreground Level   11

Background Level   7

Texture: Burlap

FILTER SETTING PARAMETERS

Foreground Level   Min **1**   Max **15**

Background Level   Min **1**   Max **15**

These images show Burlap Texture with variations in the Foreground Level and Background Level settings. See pages 202–203 for variations in Texture settings.

Foreground Level 6
Background Level 7

Foreground Level 13
Background Level 7

Foreground Level 11
Background Level 12

Foreground Level 11
Background Level 15

Foreground Level 15
Background Level 8

Foreground Level 4
Background Level 11

CONTÉ CRAYON
BURLAP (CONTINUED)

TEXTURE SETTINGS

Scaling 50%
Relief 4
Light: Top

Scaling 150%
Relief 4
Light: Top

MIXED SETTINGS

Foreground Level 11
Background Level 7

Scaling 50%
Relief 10
Light: Top

Foreground Level 5
Background Level 15

Scaling 50%
Relief 30
Light: Top

BURLAP TEXTURE SETTINGS

DEFAULT

FILTER SETTING PARAMETERS

Scaling	Min **50%**	Max **200%**
Relief	Min **0**	Max **50**

These images show variations in the Scaling and Relief Texture settings, and mixed settings of all options.

Scaling 100%
Relief 1
Light: Top

Scaling 100%
Relief 10
Light: Top

Foreground Level 5
Background Level 5

Scaling 200%
Relief 2
Light: Top

Foreground Level 15
Background Level 15

Scaling 115%
Relief 20
Light: Top

CONTÉ CRAYON
SANDSTONE

DEFAULT SANDSTONE TEXTURE

FOREGROUND LEVEL   **Foreground Level 1**
Background Level 7

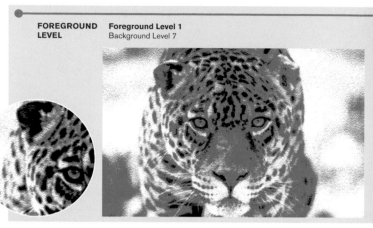

BACKGROUND LEVEL   Foreground Level 11
Background Level 1

     Foreground Level 11
Background Level 5

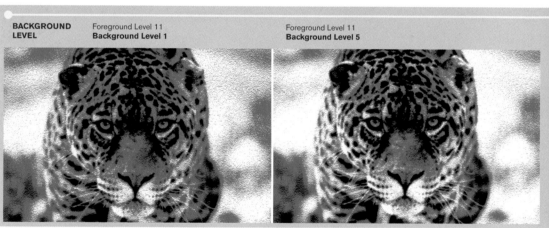

MIXED SETTINGS   **Foreground Level 8**
Background Level 8

     Foreground Level 1
Background Level 15

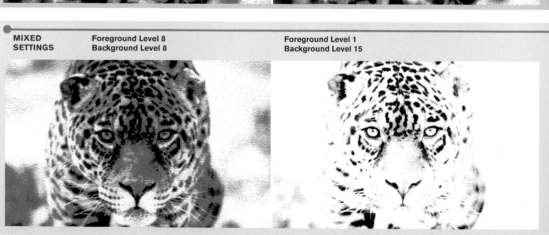

DEFAULT

Conté Crayon
Foreground Level   11
Background Level   7
Texture: Sandstone

FILTER SETTING PARAMETERS

Foreground Level   Min **1**   Max **15**

Background Level   Min **1**   Max **15**

These images show Sandstone Texture with variations in the Foreground Level and Background Level settings. See pages 206–207 for variations in Texture settings.

Foreground Level 6
Background Level 7

Foreground Level 13
Background Level 7

Foreground Level 11
Background Level 12

Foreground Level 11
Background Level 15

Foreground Level 15
Background Level 8

Foreground Level 4
Background Level 11

CONTÉ CRAYON
SANDSTONE (CONTINUED)

TEXTURE SETTINGS

Scaling 50%
Relief 4
Light: Top

Scaling 150%
Relief 4
Light: Top

MIXED SETTINGS

Foreground Level 11
Background Level 7

Scaling 50%
Relief 10
Light: Top

Foreground Level 5
Background Level 15

Scaling 50%
Relief 30
Light: Top

SANDSTONE TEXTURE SETTINGS

DEFAULT

FILTER SETTING PARAMETERS

Scaling	Min **50%**	Max **200%**
Relief	Min **0**	Max **50**

These images show variations in the Scaling and Relief Texture settings, and mixed settings of all options.

Scaling 100%
Relief 1
Light: Top

Scaling 100%
Relief 10
Light: Top

Foreground Level 5
Background Level 5

Scaling 200%
Relief 2
Light: Top

Foreground Level 15
Background Level 15

Scaling 115%
Relief 20
Light: Top

GRAPHIC PEN

DEFAULT

STROKE LENGTH	**Stroke Length 1** Light/Dark Balance 50 Stroke Direction: Right Diagonal	**Stroke Length 5** Light/Dark Balance 50 Stroke Direction: Right Diagonal

Stroke Length 15 **Light/Dark Balance 75** Stroke Direction: Right Diagonal	Stroke Length 15 **Light/Dark Balance 100** Stroke Direction: Right Diagonal

STROKE DIRECTION	Stroke Length 15 Light/Dark Balance 50 **Stroke Direction: Horizontal**

DEFAULT

Graphic Pen

Stroke Length   15

Light/Dark Balance   50

Stroke Direction: Right Diagonal

FILTER SETTING PARAMETERS

Stroke Length   Min **1**   Max **15**

Light/Dark Balance   Min **0**   Max **100**

Stroke Length 10
Light/Dark Balance 50
Stroke Direction: Right Diagonal

LIGHT/DARK BALANCE

Stroke Length 15
Light/Dark Balance 15
Stroke Direction: Right Diagonal

Stroke Length 15
Light/Dark Balance 30
Stroke Direction: Right Diagonal

Stroke Length 15
Light/Dark Balance 50
Stroke Direction: Left Diagonal

Stroke Length 15
Light/Dark Balance 50
Stroke Direction: Vertical

MIXED SETTINGS

Stroke Length 8
Light/Dark Balance 30
Stroke Direction: Right Diagonal

INTRODUCING HALFTONE PATTERN

Named after the reprographic technique that uses dots of varying sizes to replicate a continuous tone, Photoshop's Halftone Pattern goes a stage further by offering variations in the shape of the halftone pattern via the Pattern Type pull-down menu—with Line and Circle offered as alternatives to the standard Dot. Colors, as with many of the other Sketch filters, are determined by Foreground and Background Color selection.

ORIGINAL IMAGE

DEFAULT HALFTONE PATTERN
The Default settings provide an impression of how photographs appeared in early newspapers—grayscale and distinctly dotty when viewed close up. The number of dots—and therefore the level of detail—is determined by the resolution of the image. A low-resolution photograph will feature larger, more visible dots than a high-resolution shot.

Settings
Size 1
Contrast 5
Pattern Type: Dot

Foreground/
Background
Colors

EXTREME
Increasing Size and Contrast shows how the filter works. The lighter-toned sky is reproduced with smaller dots with a large amount of white space between them, while in the darker lower half the dots are larger—although at this size they are distinctly square in shape as they are represented by pixels.

Settings
Size 7
Contrast 33
Pattern Type: Dot

DEFAULT

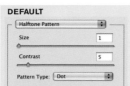

Halftone Pattern

Size 1

Contrast 5

Pattern Type: Dot

FILTER SETTING PARAMETERS

Size	Min **1**	Max **12**	
Contrast	Min **0**	Max **50**	

NEGATIVE

By simply swapping the Default Foreground and Background Colors (press x on the keyboard), a negative film effect is quickly achieved.

Settings
Size 1
Contrast 5
Pattern Type: Dot

Foreground/
Background
Colors

ORIGINAL IMAGE

Foreground/
Background
Colors

SILHOUETTE

Keeping a small dot size while increasing Contrast will fill in the darker tones, here creating a clear silhouette of the figure on the beach rendered orange against a blue background thanks to the Foreground and Background Color selection.

Settings
Size 1
Contrast 28
Pattern Type: Dot

ORIGINAL IMAGE

TV LINES

Returning to Default Foreground and Background Colors and using the Line Pattern Type with a relatively high Contrast setting recreates an old flickering, black and white television screen.

Settings
Size 3
Contrast 12
Pattern Type: Line

RADIAL CIRCLES

Setting Pattern Type to Circle introduces a concentric circular pattern, which, with a high Size setting, makes the world appear as if through the bottom of a glass.

Settings
Size 12
Contrast 7
Pattern Type: Circle

HALFTONE PATTERN

DEFAULT

SIZE

Size 3
Contrast 5
Pattern Type: Dot

Size 6
Contrast 5
Pattern Type: Dot

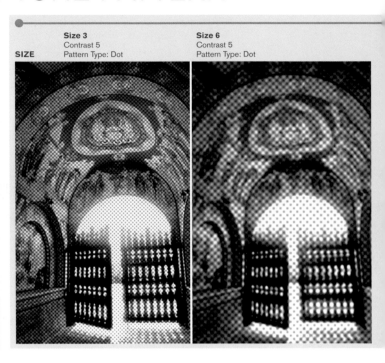

Size 1
Contrast 50
Pattern Type: Dot

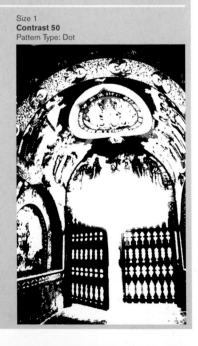

**PATTERN
TYPE**

Size 1
Contrast 5
Pattern Type: Circle

Size 1
Contrast 5
Pattern Type: Line

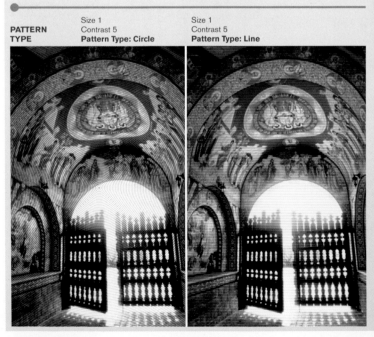

DEFAULT

FILTER SETTING PARAMETERS

Size		Min **1**	Max **12**
Contrast		Min **0**	Max **50**

Size 12
Contrast 5
Pattern Type: Dot

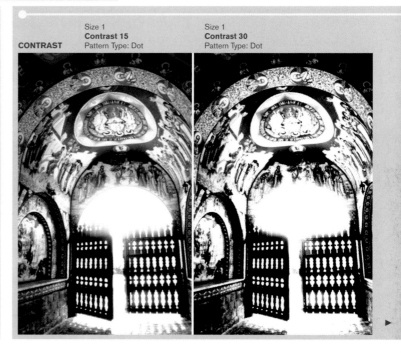

CONTRAST

Size 1
Contrast 15
Pattern Type: Dot

Size 1
Contrast 30
Pattern Type: Dot

▶

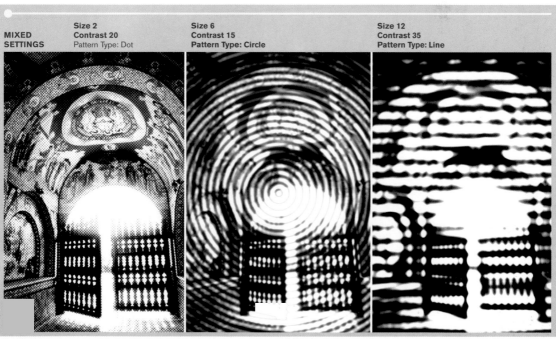

MIXED SETTINGS

Size 2
Contrast 20
Pattern Type: Dot

Size 6
Contrast 15
Pattern Type: Circle

Size 12
Contrast 35
Pattern Type: Line

NOTE PAPER

DEFAULT

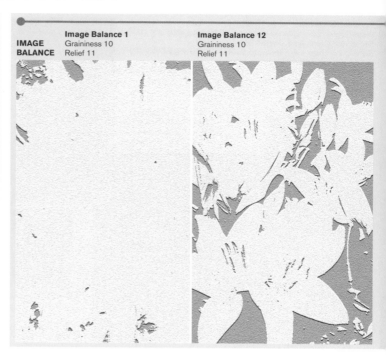

IMAGE BALANCE

Image Balance 1
Graininess 10
Relief 11

Image Balance 12
Graininess 10
Relief 11

Image Balance 25
Graininess 20
Relief 11

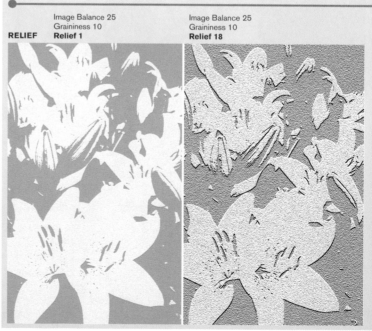

RELIEF

Image Balance 25
Graininess 10
Relief 1

Image Balance 25
Graininess 10
Relief 18

DEFAULT

Note Paper	⬍
Image Balance	25
Graininess	10
Relief	11

FILTER SETTING PARAMETERS

Image Balance	Min **0**	Max **50**	
Graininess	Min **0**	Max **20**	
Relief	Min **0**	Max **25**	

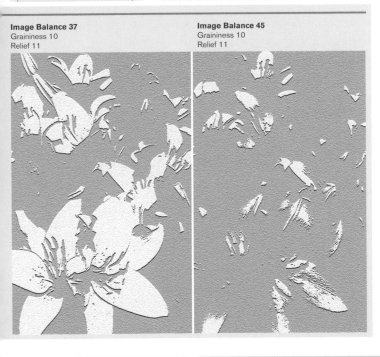

Image Balance 37
Graininess 10
Relief 11

Image Balance 45
Graininess 10
Relief 11

GRAININESS

Image Balance 25
Graininess 1
Relief 11

Image Balance 25
Graininess 10
Relief 25

MIXED SETTINGS

Image Balance 35
Graininess 1
Relief 20

Image Balance 14
Graininess 20
Relief 2

INTRODUCING PHOTOCOPY

The Photocopy filter initially appears to work much like the other Sketch filters by primarily seeking out edges—however, the filter surprises with the subtlety of tone it produces with certain images, so that in places an image can have a near continuous-tone photographic quality. It's an unusual mix of strongly defined line work with carefully considered shading.

ORIGINAL IMAGE

DEFAULT PHOTOCOPY
Against such a clear uncluttered background, the skater's outline is naturally clearly defined, but on close inspection the face, hands, and clothing contain a surprising pencil sketch quality.

Settings
Detail 7
Darkness 8

Foreground/
Background
Colors

MAXIMUM DETAIL
Maximizing Detail initially increases the contrast to the point that many of the darker tones fill in and lose detail, but these can be retrieved by reducing Darkness, resulting in an even stronger photographic quality.

Settings
Detail 24
Darkness 2

DEFAULT

Photocopy	
Detail	7
Darkness	8

FILTER SETTING PARAMETERS

Detail	Min 1	Max 24
Darkness	Min 1	Max 50

ORIGINAL IMAGE

SUMI-E
With the appropriate subject matter, and with settings that maximize detail but keep contrast low, a convincing sumi-e (oriental ink and wash technique) is the result.

Settings
Detail 24
Darkness 3

LINE ARTWORK
Almost reversing the settings hardens the outlines and increases the contrast to the point that the image becomes line artwork with no subtlety of shading.

Settings
Detail 1
Darkness 50

ORIGINAL IMAGE

BLUEPRINT
Choosing an appropriate dark blue for the Background Color, setting the Foreground Color to white, and ensuring a strong clear line with a low Detail setting and a high Darkness setting creates an architect's blueprint.

Settings
Detail 1
Darkness 50

Foreground/
Background Colors

Foreground/
Background Colors

RED PEN
Reverting to white Background Color against a bold Foreground Color creates a distinctive clean outline. Increasing Detail a little introduces some texture.

Settings
Detail 6
Darkness 50

PHOTOCOPY

DEFAULT

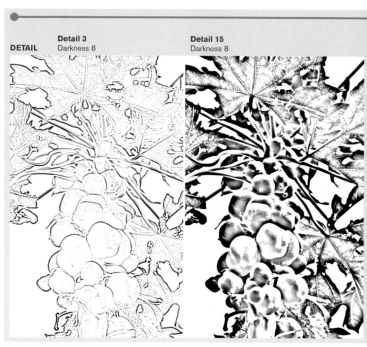

DETAIL

Detail 3
Darkness 8

Detail 15
Darkness 8

Detail 7
Darkness 50

MIXED SETTINGS

Detail 20
Darkness 30

Detail 1
Darkness 50

DEFAULT

Photocopy	▼
Detail	7
Darkness	8

FILTER SETTING PARAMETERS

| Detail | Min **1** | Max **24** |
| Darkness | Min **1** | Max **50** |

Detail 24
Darkness 8

DARKNESS

Detail 7
Darkness 2

Detail 7
Darkness 25

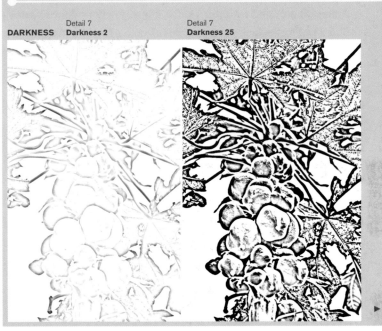

Detail 20
Darkness 3

Detail 24
Darkness 50

Detail 5
Darkness 5

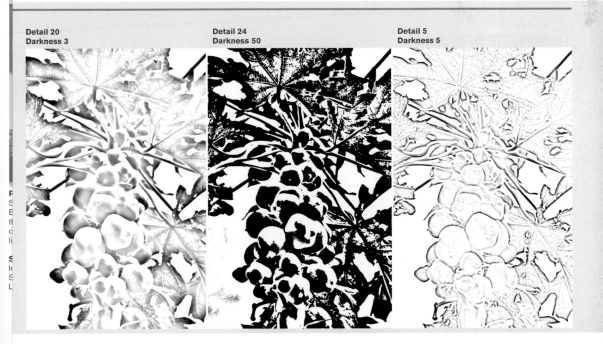

PLASTER

DEFAULT

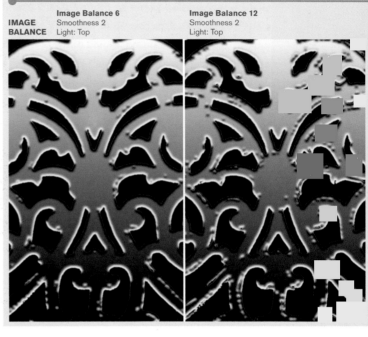

IMAGE BALANCE

Image Balance 6
Smoothness 2
Light: Top

Image Balance 12
Smoothness 2
Light: Top

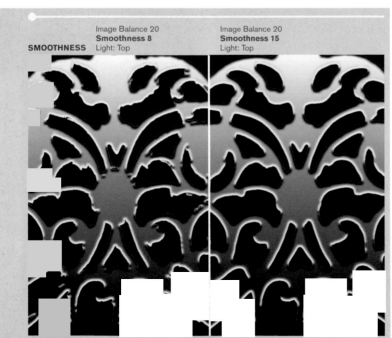

SMOOTHNESS

Image Balance 20
Smoothness 8
Light: Top

Image Balance 20
Smoothness 15
Light: Top

MIXED SETTINGS

Image Balance 15
Smoothness 10
Light: Right

DEFAULT

Plaster

Image Balance 20

Smoothness 2

Light: Top

FILTER SETTING PARAMETERS

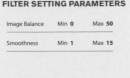

Image Balance	Min **0**	Max **50**
Smoothness	Min **1**	Max **15**

Image Balance 30
Smoothness 2
Light: Top

Image Balance 35
Smoothness 2
Light: Top

Image Balance 40
Smoothness 2
Light: Top

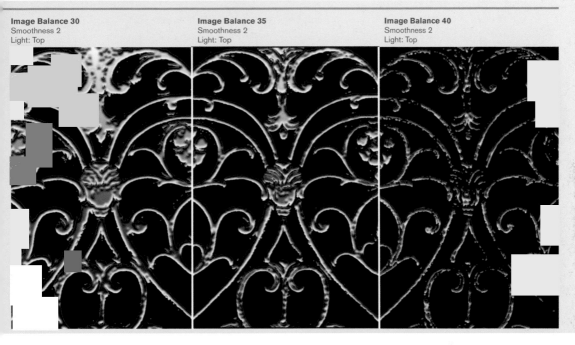

Image Balance 23
Smoothness 1
Light: Left

Image Balance 30
Smoothness 10
Light: Top Right

Image Balance 35
Smoothness 10
Light: Left

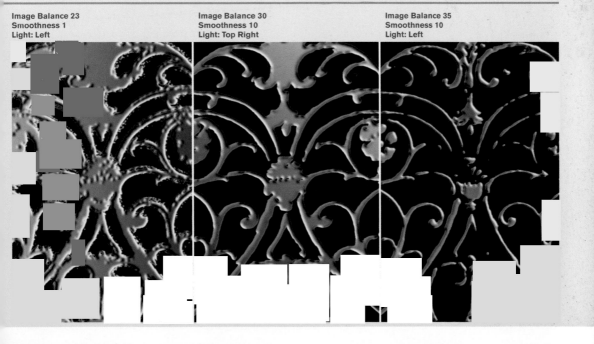

INTRODUCING RETICULATION

Reticulation is a pre-digital photography term that refers to cracks or wrinkles appearing in film emulsion—usually due to incorrect film processing technique but something that was experimented with deliberately. Photoshop's digital version offers three sets of controls, with the Density slider determining the faux reticulation effect.

ORIGINAL IMAGE

DEFAULT RETICULATION
The reticulation pattern is more prominent the lower the resolution of the image, but at Default setting the filter will usually apply a clearly visible, random texture over the image.

Settings
Density 12
Foreground Level 40
Background Level 5

Foreground/
Background
Colors

LOW CONTRAST
With default black and white Foreground and Background Colors minimizing the Foreground Level (black) and maximizing the Background Level (white), a low contrast results.

Settings
Density 8
Foreground Level 0
Background Level 50

DEFAULT

Reticulation	
Density	12
Foreground Level	40
Background Level	5

FILTER SETTING PARAMETERS

Density	Min 0	Max 50
Foreground Level	Min 0	Max 50
Background Level	Min 0	Max 50

GRAPHIC

Setting both Foreground and Background Levels to 50 creates a strong graphic result with only the reticulation pattern adding any tonal variation.

Settings
Density 30
Foreground Level 50
Background Level 50

ORIGINAL IMAGE

Foreground/
Background
Colors

NEGATIVE

Press the x key to invert the default Foreground and Background Colors to create the negative reticulation, while evening up Foreground Level and Background Level controls introduces some additional tonal information.

Settings
Density 30
Foreground Level 32
Background Level 18

ORIGINAL IMAGE

BOLD COLORS

Using two bold colors produces a bright, powerful result; perhaps counterintuitively reducing the Foreground Level control increases detail in the image.

Settings
Density 42
Foreground Level 17
Background Level 50

Foreground/
Background
Colors

PASTEL SHADES

A pale Foreground Color produces a light airy image with the Reticulation pattern reinforcing the texture.

Settings
Density 30
Foreground Level 14
Background Level 16

RETICULATION

DEFAULT

DENSITY

Density 4
Foreground Level 40
Background Level 5

Density 30
Foreground Level 40
Background Level 5

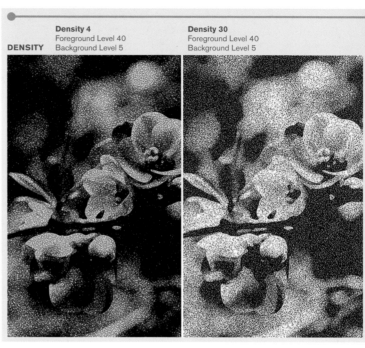

**MIXED
SETTINGS**

**Density 50
Foreground Level 10
Background Level 0**

**Density 5
Foreground Level 50**
Background Level 5

**Density 1
Foreground Level 10
Background Level 10**

DEFAULT

Reticulation

Density	12
Foreground Level	40
Background Level	5

FILTER SETTING PARAMETERS

Density	Min **0**	Max **50**
Foreground Level	Min **0**	Max **50**
Background Level	Min **0**	Max **50**

Density 50
Foreground Level 40
Background Level 5

FOREGROUND LEVEL

Density 12
Foreground Level 5
Background Level 5

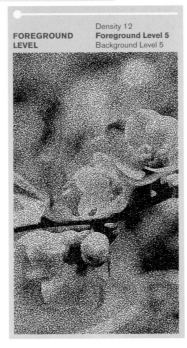

BACKGROUND LEVEL

Density 12
Foreground Level 40
Background Level 30

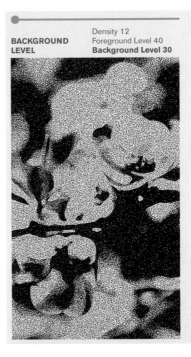

Density 0
Foreground Level 50
Background Level 50

Density 40
Foreground Level 20
Background Level 10

Density 0
Foreground Level 40
Background Level 20

INTRODUCING STAMP

Stamp is a straightforward yet graphically powerful filter when used with an appropriate image. Named after the flat, monotone images created by wooden or rubber stamps, the filter has two levels of control. Light/Dark Balance controls the Foreground and Background Color distribution, while Smoothness determines the level of edge simplification.

DEFAULT STAMP
With the default settings applied, the result is a high-contrast, black and white image in which the outline of the eagle and a few feathers, but little else, are discernible.

Settings
Light/Dark Balance 25
Smoothness 5

ORIGINAL IMAGE

Foreground/
Background
Colors

INCREASING DETAIL
Moving Light/Dark Balance toward the left increases the Background Color distribution, in this case default white, and combined with a minimum smoothness setting reveals much more detail.

Settings
Light/Dark Balance 8
Smoothness 1

DEFAULT

Stamp	
Light/Dark Balance	25
Smoothness	5

FILTER SETTING PARAMETERS

Light/Dark Balance Min **0**   Max **50**

Smoothness   Min **1**   Max **50**

ORIGINAL IMAGE

Foreground/
Background
Colors

BLURRED EDGES
Increasing the Smoothness
setting radically blurs the
edges, but with the simple,
distinctive shapes in this
image, a pleasing graphic
is created.

Settings
Light/Dark Balance 23
Smoothness 16

BLUE STAMP
Sampling the Foreground
Color from the blue sky
creates a blue and white
image, here with good
detail due to minimum
Smoothness and with
Light/Dark Balance set
to maximize the white
Background Color.

Settings
Light/Dark Balance 1
Smoothness 1

ORIGINAL IMAGE

Foreground/
Background
Colors

PURPLE MOTIF
Selecting some alternative
Foreground and Background
Colors, and adjusting the
Light/Dark Balance and
Smoothness sliders, creates
elegant motifs.

Settings
Light/Dark Balance 45
Smoothness 1

TWO TONES
Although not physically
possible with a single rubber
stamp, with a digital Stamp
filter sampling two colors
from an image and applying
them as the Foreground and
Background Colors yields
simple yet effective results.

Foreground/
Background
Colors

Settings
Light/Dark Balance 42
Smoothness 4

STAMP

DEFAULT

Light/Dark Balance 10
Smoothness 5

Light/Dark Balance 40
Smoothness 5

**MIXED
SETTINGS**

Light/Dark Balance 1
Smoothness 1

Light/Dark Balance 20
Smoothness 30

Light/Dark Balance 5
Smoothness 1

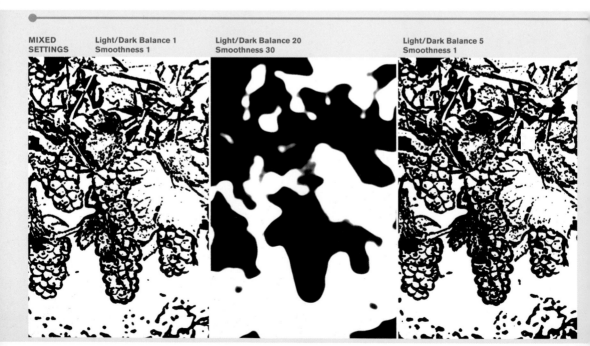

DEFAULT

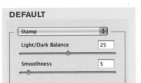

Stamp
Light/Dark Balance   25
Smoothness   5

FILTER SETTING PARAMETERS

Light/Dark Balance Min **0**   Max **50**

Smoothness   Min **1**   Max **50**

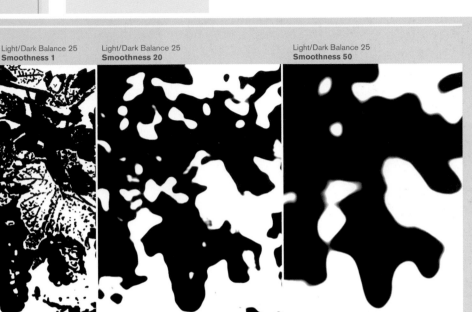

SMOOTHNESS

Light/Dark Balance 25
Smoothness 1

Light/Dark Balance 25
Smoothness 20

Light/Dark Balance 25
Smoothness 50

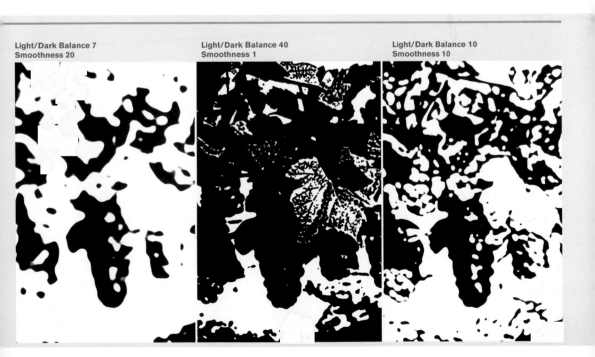

Light/Dark Balance 7
Smoothness 20

Light/Dark Balance 40
Smoothness 1

Light/Dark Balance 10
Smoothness 10

INTRODUCING TORN EDGES

Although there are some workarounds that provide a more convincing "torn edge" effect, the Torn Edges filter is still capable of creating a wide variety of effects. It shares the same Smoothness control as the Stamp filter, and has Image Balance, which governs the overall tone of the image—but Torn Edges features a third setting, Contrast, which as well as the obvious also simulates a grain effect at its maximum setting.

ORIGINAL IMAGE

INCREASED EXPOSURE
Moving the Image Balance to the left lightens the image as if increasing the exposure, while reducing contrast adds tonal variation. Increasing Smoothness reduces the fuzziness and sharpens the image.

Settings
Image Balance 18
Smoothness 14
Contrast 1

DEFAULT TORN EDGES
The Torn Edges filter seeks out high-contrast edges, and with this image using the default settings, gives them a fuzzy appearance. The default settings also create a stark black and white image with default Foreground and Background Colors of black and white.

Settings
Image Balance 25
Smoothness 11
Contrast 17

Foreground/
Background
Colors

DEFAULT

Torn Edges	
Image Balance	25
Smoothness	11
Contrast	17

FILTER SETTING PARAMETERS

	Min	Max
Image Balance	0	50
Smoothness	1	15
Contrast	1	25

ORIGINAL IMAGE

HAUNTED
Simply inverting the default Foreground and Background Colors (by pressing x) creates an instant negative, and with careful adjustment of the filter's controls, a surreal, ghostly effect is achieved.

Settings
Image Balance 20
Smoothness 12
Contrast 2

TORN EDGES
With a low Smoothness setting applied, the "torn edge" effect becomes more apparent, particularly along the long, contrasting edges of the trees.

Settings
Image Balance 12
Smoothness 3
Contrast 16

ORIGINAL IMAGE

Foreground/
Background
Colors

SEPIA
With appropriate Foreground and Background Colors, it's possible to recreate a vintage, sepia-toned effect, with a moderate Smoothness setting to reinforce an historical, fuzzy quality.

Settings
Image Balance 17
Smoothness 9
Contrast 1

VIBRANT
Sampling bright Foreground and Background Colors from the image and increasing the Smoothness and Contrast produces a vibrant, colorful graphic.

Foreground/
Background
Colors

Settings
Image Balance 17
Smoothness 15
Contrast 14

TORN EDGES

DEFAULT

IMAGE BALANCE

Image Balance 13
Smoothness 11
Contrast 17

Image Balance 32
Smoothness 11
Contrast 17

Image Balance 25
Smoothness 15
Contrast 17

CONTRAST

Image Balance 25
Smoothness 11
Contrast 1

Image Balance 25
Smoothness 11
Contrast 9

DEFAULT

Torn Edges

Image Balance 25
Smoothness 11
Contrast 17

FILTER SETTING PARAMETERS

Image Balance	Min **0**	Max **50**
Smoothness	Min **1**	Max **15**
Contrast	Min **1**	Max **25**

Image Balance 40
Smoothness 11
Contrast 17

SMOOTHNESS

Image Balance 25
Smoothness 1
Contrast 17

Image Balance 25
Smoothness 6
Contrast 17

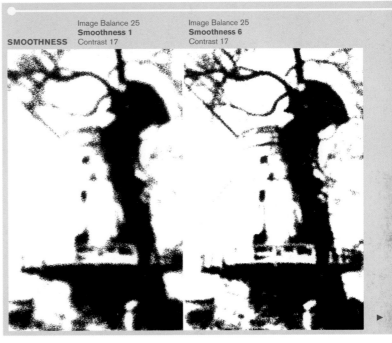

Image Balance 25
Smoothness 11
Contrast 25

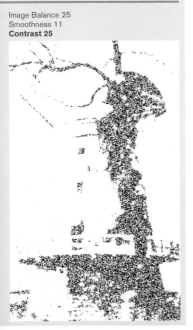

**MIXED
SETTINGS**

Image Balance 18
Smoothness 5
Contrast 1

Image Balance 33
Smoothness 15
Contrast 22

INTRODUCING WATER PAPER

Photoshop's Water Paper filter is the only filter in the Sketch collection that renders an image in color, and as such is not affected by the Foreground and Background Colors. The filter attempts to replicate a watercolor painting and is an alternative to the Watercolor filter found in Artistic filters. The key control is Fiber Length, which attempts to reproduce the effect of watercolor paint collecting and merging in the gaps in highly textured art paper.

ORIGINAL IMAGE

DEFAULT WATER PAPER
With the default Fiber Length setting of 15, the colors visibly "bleed" into one another along the axes of the virtual art paper.

Settings
Fiber Length 15
Brightness 60
Contrast 80

POP ART
Although not the filter's intended purpose, setting a low Fiber Length while increasing Brightness and Contrast to near maximum produces a bright pop art effect.

Settings
Fiber Length 3
Brightness 88
Contrast 83

DEFAULT

Water Paper

Fiber Length	15
Brightness	60
Contrast	80

FILTER SETTING PARAMETERS

Fiber Length	Min 3	Max 50
Brightness	Min 0	Max 100
Contrast	Min 0	Max 100

PASTEL
Combining a low Fiber Length setting with low Contrast gives the image a pastel-like quality.

Settings
Fiber Length 9
Brightness 60
Contrast 20

EXTRA BLEED
Increasing the Fiber Length setting to increase the bleed effect darkens the image. This can be partly reversed by increasing Brightness, but watch for blown highlights.

Settings
Fiber Length 30
Brightness 52
Contrast 83

ORIGINAL IMAGE

ORIGINAL IMAGE

ABSTRACT
Setting maximum Fiber Length renders this particular image into a colorful, futuristic abstract.

Settings
Fiber Length 50
Brightness 54
Contrast 70

WATERCOLOR
The filter's intended purpose—to replicate a watercolor painting—has worked relatively successfully with this nighttime cityscape.

Settings
Fiber Length 6
Brightness 61
Contrast 37

WATER PAPER

DEFAULT

**FIBER
LENGTH**

Fiber Length 3
Brightness 60
Contrast 80

Fiber Length 35
Brightness 60
Contrast 80

Fiber Length 15
Brightness 100
Contrast 80

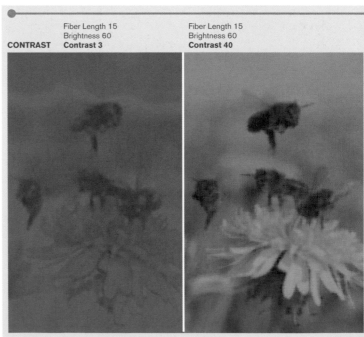

CONTRAST

Fiber Length 15
Brightness 60
Contrast 3

Fiber Length 15
Brightness 60
Contrast 40

DEFAULT

Water Paper

Fiber Length 15
Brightness 60
Contrast 80

FILTER SETTING PARAMETERS

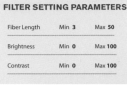

Fiber Length	Min **3**	Max **50**
Brightness	Min **0**	Max **100**
Contrast	Min **0**	Max **100**

Fiber Length 50
Brightness 60
Contrast 80

BRIGHTNESS

Fiber Length 15
Brightness 30
Contrast 80

Fiber Length 15
Brightness 80
Contrast 80

Fiber Length 15
Brightness 60
Contrast 90

**MIXED
SETTINGS**

Fiber Length 5
Brightness 60
Contrast 90

Fiber Length 50
Brightness 50
Contrast 60

STYLIZE FILTERS

There is a fantastic range of striking effects you can generate with the Stylize filters, but there is only one in the Photoshop Filter Gallery—the Glowing Edges filter. The other eight Stylize filters can be found in Other Filter Effects on pages 392–405. Use them with the techniques outlined in The Scope of Filters, pages 292–325, to leave more of the image intact.

INTRODUCING GLOWING EDGES

Glowing Edges is one of the most striking and colorful of all Photoshop's filters. From a technical perspective, the filter seeks out edges and duplicates them with another using adjacent colors, inverting the result. With three controls to experiment with, Glowing Edges produces an array of colorful effects—but the filter should be handled with care.

ORIGINAL IMAGE

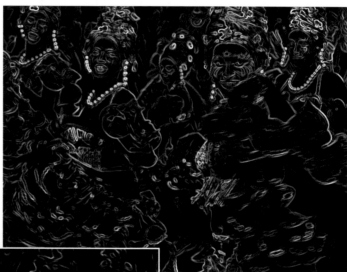

DEFAULT GLOWING EDGES
With plenty of colors and edges to work with on this image, default Glowing Edges settings produce the characteristic vivid line work on a black background.

Settings
Edge Width 2
Edge Brightness 6
Smoothness 5

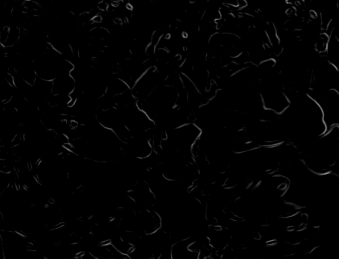

SIMPLIFY EDGES
Increasing the Smoothness setting progressively removes edges, starting with the least contrasting. At maximum setting, only the most contrasting lines decipher the image.

Settings
Edge Width 2
Edge Brightness 5
Smoothness 15

DEFAULT

Glowing Edges	
Edge Width	2
Edge Brightness	6
Smoothness	5

FILTER SETTING PARAMETERS

Edge Width	Min **1**	Max **14**
Edge Brightness	Min **0**	Max **20**
Smoothness	Min **1**	Max **15**

HYPER DETAIL

Minimum Edge Width and near minimum Smoothness settings combine with maximum Edge Brightness to create a hypersurreal world of bright, glowing edges.

Settings
Edge Width 1
Edge Brightness 20
Smoothness 2

SMOOTH AND SUBDUED

The only way to calm the filter down is to set maximum Edge Width with near minimum Edge Brightness for neon pastel outlines.

ORIGINAL IMAGE

Settings
Edge Width 14
Edge Brightness 1
Smoothness 9

SIMPLE OUTLINE

Simple shapes against a plain background can create effective, glowing outline artwork.

Settings
Edge Width 10
Edge Brightness 4
Smoothness 15

ORIGINAL IMAGE

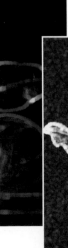

BLOCKY

The pixelated texture on the apples and in the background is due to the relatively low resolution of this 1.5-megapixel image.

Settings
Edge Width 6
Edge Brightness 15
Smoothness 3

GLOWING EDGES

DEFAULT

EDGE WIDTH

Edge Width 5
Edge Brightness 6
Smoothness 5

Edge Width 10
Edge Brightness 6
Smoothness 5

Edge Width 2
Edge Brightness 10
Smoothness 5

Edge Width 2
Edge Brightness 15
Smoothness 5

Edge Width 2
Edge Brightness 20
Smoothness 5

MIXED SETTINGS

Edge Width 1
Edge Brightness 10
Smoothness 5

Edge Width 10
Edge Brightness 1
Smoothness 5

Edge Width 10
Edge Brightness 10
Smoothness 5

DEFAULT

Glowing Edges
Edge Width   2
Edge Brightness   6
Smoothness   5

FILTER SETTING PARAMETERS

Edge Width	Min	**1**	Max	**14**
Edge Brightness	Min	**0**	Max	**20**
Smoothness	Min	**1**	Max	**15**

Edge Width 14
Edge Brightness 6
Smoothness 5

EDGE BRIGHTNESS

Edge Width 2
Edge Brightness 1
Smoothness 5

Edge Width 2
Edge Brightness 3
Smoothness 5

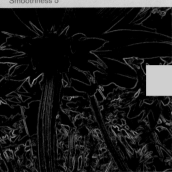

SMOOTHNESS

Edge Width 2
Edge Brightness 6
Smoothness 1

Edge Width 2
Edge Brightness 6
Smoothness 10

Edge Width 2
Edge Brightness 6
Smoothness 15

Edge Width 1
Edge Brightness 15
Smoothness 1

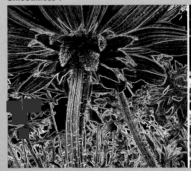

Edge Width 7
Edge Brightness 8
Smoothness 14

Edge Width 2
Edge Brightness 20
Smoothness 15

TEXTURE FILTERS

As their name suggests, the Texture filters create a series of textures that can be applied to images to make them appear as though they've been created on burlap or canvas, or even with a suggestion of stained glass. You'll find that the settings can subdue the textures so they appear as a subtle overlay rather than dominating or distorting the image, which can happen if the texture is too strongly applied.

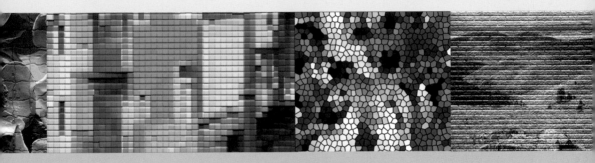

	PAGE

INTRODUCING CRAQUELURE

Named after the distinctive cracked pattern found on numerous oil paintings of the 18th and 19th centuries—caused by the paint or varnish contracting and cracking over time—Photoshop's filter works by laying a seemingly random pattern over the image. Crack Spacing control determines the size of the pattern so that you can set the filter to an appropriate size for most image resolutions.

ORIGINAL IMAGE

DEFAULT CRAQUELURE
On closer inspection, it's possible to detect how the cracking pattern, rather than being randomly applied by filter, is in fact displaced by the tonal changes in the image.

Settings
Crack Spacing 15
Crack Depth 6
Crack Brightness 9

3D EFFECT
Setting both Crack Spacing and Crack Depth to the maximum settings, while making the cracking as dark as possible with Crack Brightness 0, shows how the filter applies dark lines to certain high-contrasting edges, notably around the edges of some of the frozen leaf margins, giving them a 3D or drop-shadow appearance.

Settings
Crack Spacing 100
Crack Depth 10
Crack Brightness 0

DEFAULT

Craquelure	
Crack Spacing	15
Crack Depth	6
Crack Brightness	9

FILTER SETTING PARAMETERS

Crack Spacing	Min 2	Max 100
Crack Depth	Min 0	Max 10
Crack Brightness	Min 0	Max 10

ORIGINAL IMAGE

PLASTIC CRACKS
Setting a high Crack Spacing (depending on the image resolution) and the maximum Crack Depth and low Crack Brightness gives the image a plastic appearance.

Settings
Crack Spacing 100
Crack Depth 10
Crack Brightness 2

REALISTIC CRAQUELURE
Achieving a realistic craquelure effect is impossible with a one-pass filter; however, a low Crack Depth and high Crack Brightness will usually provide the best result.

Settings
Crack Spacing 11
Crack Depth 2
Crack Brightness 10

ORIGINAL IMAGE

Settings
Crack Spacing 2
Crack Depth 5
Crack Brightness 9

WATERCOLOR
Certain images, landscapes with cloudy skies for example, can take on the appearance of a watercolor when a very low Crack Spacing is set (above). Reducing the Crack Depth has lightened the image (left).

Settings
Crack Spacing 2
Crack Depth 0
Crack Brightness 9

CRAQUELURE

DEFAULT

CRACK SPACING

Crack Spacing 2
Crack Depth 6
Crack Brightness 9

Crack Spacing 5
Crack Depth 6
Crack Brightness 9

Crack Spacing 100
Crack Depth 6
Crack Brightness 9

CRACK DEPTH

Crack Spacing 15
Crack Depth 1
Crack Brightness 9

Crack Spacing 15
Crack Depth 10
Crack Brightness 9

Crack Spacing 80
Crack Depth 10
Crack Brightness 9

Crack Spacing 60
Crack Depth 10
Crack Brightness 1

Crack Spacing 10
Crack Depth 1
Crack Brightness 0

DEFAULT

Craquelure	
Crack Spacing	15
Crack Depth	6
Crack Brightness	9

FILTER SETTING PARAMETERS

Crack Spacing	Min **2**	Max **100**
Crack Depth	Min **0**	Max **10**
Crack Brightness	Min **0**	Max **10**

Crack Spacing 9
Crack Depth 6
Crack Brightness 9

Crack Spacing 25
Crack Depth 6
Crack Brightness 9

Crack Spacing 50
Crack Depth 6
Crack Brightness 9

▶

CRACK BRIGHTNESS

Crack Spacing 15
Crack Depth 6
Crack Brightness 0

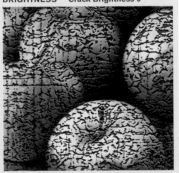

MIXED SETTINGS

Crack Spacing 5
Crack Depth 1
Crack Brightness 9

Crack Spacing 40
Crack Depth 1
Crack Brightness 9

▶

Crack Spacing 30
Crack Depth 10
Crack Brightness 5

Crack Spacing 100
Crack Depth 3
Crack Brightness 0

Crack Spacing 75
Crack Depth 2
Crack Brightness 10

INTRODUCING GRAIN

Certain types of conventional film stock—notably the more sensitive or "faster" black and white types—became famous for their "grainy" texture, which many photographers felt added atmosphere to their images. The grainy pattern is caused by metallic particles in the film's emulsion. There are ten different types of grain available in Photoshop's Grain filter, each of which can be fine-tuned using the Intensity and Contrast settings.

ORIGINAL IMAGE

DEFAULT GRAIN
For purposes of authenticity, the source image was converted to a grayscale image before applying the default Grain settings. The filter creates a pleasing, grainy, speckled pattern that adds to the misty atmosphere of the shot.

Settings
Intensity 40
Contrast 50
Grain Type: Regular

COLOR GRAIN
The original color shot again with the default Regular Grain Type applied also takes on a speckled, grainy appearance—increased due to a higher Intensity setting—but is less atmospheric than the black and white version above.

Settings
Intensity 71
Contrast 50
Grain Type: Regular

ORIGINAL IMAGE

DEFAULT

Grain	
Intensity	40
Contrast	50
Grain Type:	Regular

FILTER SETTING PARAMETERS

Intensity	Min **0**	Max **100**
Contrast	Min **0**	Max **100**

INCREASED CONTRAST

As well as applying a grain texture—Soft in this example—the filter's Contrast control also helps to reinforce a harsher, more "rough and ready" effect.

Settings
Intensity 41
Contrast 73
Grain Type: Soft

ORIGINAL IMAGE

INK OUTLINE

Although it has no bearing on traditional grain, the Speckle Type creates an illustrative effect by adding a distinctive dark outline to contrasting edges.

Settings
Intensity 9
Contrast 65
Grain Type: Speckle

HORIZONTAL AND VERTICAL

Again, having no resemblance to traditional grain doesn't prevent the Horizontal (left) and Vertical (below) Grain Types from creating powerful graphic images. Experimenting with the Intensity and Contrast controls pays dividends.

Settings
Intensity 86
Contrast 10
Grain Type: Horizontal

Settings
Intensity 51
Contrast 90
Grain Type: Vertical

ORIGINAL IMAGE

GRAIN

DEFAULT

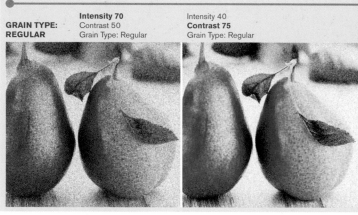

GRAIN TYPE:
REGULAR

Intensity 70
Contrast 50
Grain Type: Regular

Intensity 40
Contrast 75
Grain Type: Regular

GRAIN TYPE:
SPRINKLES

Intensity 40
Contrast 50
Grain Type: Sprinkles

Intensity 25
Contrast 25
Grain Type: Sprinkles

Intensity 50
Contrast 100
Grain Type: Sprinkles

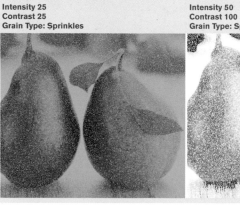

GRAIN TYPE:
CONTRASTY

Intensity 40
Contrast 50
Grain Type: Contrasty

Intensity 25
Contrast 25
Grain Type: Contrasty

Intensity 50
Contrast 100
Grain Type: Contrasty

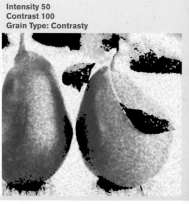

DEFAULT

Grain
Intensity 40
Contrast 50
Grain Type: Regular

FILTER SETTING PARAMETERS

Intensity   Min **0**   Max **100**

Contrast   Min **0**   Max **100**

**GRAIN TYPE:
SOFT**

Intensity 40
Contrast 50
Grain Type: Soft

Intensity 100
Contrast 25
Grain Type: Soft

Intensity 75
Contrast 75
Grain Type: Soft

**GRAIN TYPE:
CLUMPED**

Intensity 40
Contrast 50
Grain Type: Clumped

Intensity 100
Contrast 25
Grain Type: Clumped

Intensity 75
Contrast 75
Grain Type: Clumped

**GRAIN TYPE:
ENLARGED**

Intensity 40
Contrast 50
Grain Type: Enlarged

Intensity 100
Contrast 25
Grain Type: Enlarged

Intensity 75
Contrast 75
Grain Type: Enlarged

GRAIN (CONTINUED)

**GRAIN TYPE:
STIPPLED**

Intensity 40
Contrast 50
Grain Type: Stippled

Intensity 25
Contrast 25
Grain Type: Stippled

Intensity 50
Contrast 100
Grain Type: Stippled

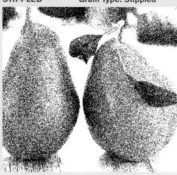

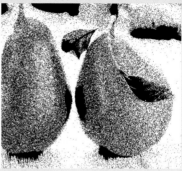

**GRAIN TYPE:
VERTICAL**

Intensity 40
Contrast 50
Grain Type: Vertical

Intensity 25
Contrast 25
Grain Type: Vertical

Intensity 50
Contrast 100
Grain Type: Vertical

**MIXED
SETTINGS**

Intensity 50
Contrast 100
Grain Type: Soft

Intensity 50
Contrast 100
Grain Type: Enlarged

Intensity 100
Contrast 100
Grain Type: Horizontal

DEFAULT

FILTER SETTING PARAMETERS

Intensity	Min **0**	Max **100**
Contrast	Min **0**	Max **100**

**GRAIN TYPE:
HORIZONTAL**

Intensity 40
Contrast 50
Grain Type: Horizontal

Intensity 100
Contrast 25
Grain Type: Horizontal

Intensity 75
Contrast 75
Grain Type: Horizontal

**GRAIN TYPE:
SPECKLED**

Intensity 40
Contrast 50
Grain Type: Speckled

Intensity 100
Contrast 25
Grain Type: Speckled

Intensity 75
Contrast 75
Grain Type: Speckled

**Intensity 100
Contrast 100
Grain Type: Vertical**

**Intensity 100
Contrast 0
Grain Type: Stippled**

**Intensity 100
Contrast 0
Grain Type: Speckled**

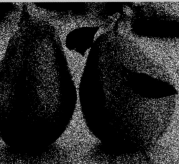

INTRODUCING MOSAIC TILES

Mosaic Tiles, on first impression, is reminiscent of the Craquelure filter (see pages 252–255); however, the pattern laid down by Mosaic Tiles is not affected by the tonal values of the image. Although the filter doesn't replicate a true mosaic, in which each individual tile or *tessera* is a uniform color, the Mosaic Tiles filter can recreate a convincing mosaic look as well as produce some of its own unique digital interpretations.

ORIGINAL IMAGE

DEFAULT MOSAIC TILES
With the right image, the default settings produce a credible result, although "tiles" of two or more colors give the game away.

Settings
Tile Size 12
Grout Width 3
Lighten Grout 9

CRAQUELURE
With a minimum Grout Width setting and an appropriate Tile Size, the Mosaic Tiles filter in many ways replicates a more convincing craquelure effect than the Craquelure filter.

Settings
Tile Size 5
Grout Width 1
Lighten Grout 9

DEFAULT

Mosaic Tiles	
Tile Size	12
Grout Width	3
Lighten Grout	9

FILTER SETTING PARAMETERS

	Min	Max
Tile Size	2	100
Grout Width	1	15
Lighten Grout	0	10

ORIGINAL IMAGE

SIZE AND SHAPE
Interestingly, as the Tile Size increases the tiles become more uniform in shape. Compare the shape in the large-tile image right with that of the small-tile image far right. The impact of the Tile Size setting on the scale of the tiles is governed by the image's resolution. With a high-resolution image, the Tile Size needs to be set high for the pattern to be discernible.

Settings
Tile Size 100
Grout Width 1
Lighten Grout 0

Settings
Tile Size 10
Grout Width 1
Lighten Grout 0

ORIGINAL IMAGE

TINY TILES
Retaining maximum Grout Width and setting a small Tile Size so that there's more grout than tile creates an irregular spotty effect.

Settings
Tile Size 9
Grout Width 15
Lighten Grout 6

MAXIMUM GROUT
Some of the most interesting effects occur when Grout Width is set to maximum—recreating a shower mat look when the grout (the material used between the tiles in conventional tiling) is set at its lightest.

Settings
Tile Size 43
Grout Width 15
Lighten Grout 10

MOSAIC TILES

DEFAULT

TILE SIZE

Tile Size 2
Grout Width 3
Lighten Grout 9

Tile Size 6
Grout Width 3
Lighten Grout 9

GROUT WIDTH

Tile Size 12
Grout Width 1
Lighten Grout 9

Tile Size 12
Grout Width 5
Lighten Grout 9

Tile Size 12
Grout Width 10
Lighten Grout 9

Tile Size 50
Grout Width 1
Lighten Grout 0

Tile Size 5
Grout Width 10
Lighten Grout 5

Tile Size 25
Grout Width 15
Lighten Grout 5

DEFAULT

Mosaic Tiles

Tile Size	12
Grout Width	3
Lighten Grout	9

FILTER SETTING PARAMETERS

Tile Size	Min 2	Max 100
Grout Width	Min 1	Max 15
Lighten Grout	Min 0	Max 10

Tile Size 20
Grout Width 3
Lighten Grout 9

Tile Size 50
Grout Width 3
Lighten Grout 9

Tile Size 100
Grout Width 3
Lighten Grout 9

LIGHTEN GROUT

Tile Size 12
Grout Width 3
Lighten Grout 0

Tile Size 12
Grout Width 3
Lighten Grout 5

MIXED SETTINGS

**Tile Size 2
Grout Width 1
Lighten Grout 0**

**Tile Size 50
Grout Width 6
Lighten Grout 2**

**Tile Size 100
Grout Width 10
Lighten Grout 0**

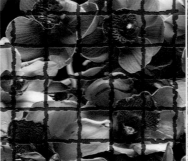

**Tile Size 8
Grout Width 6
Lighten Grout 7**

INTRODUCING PATCHWORK

The success or otherwise of the Patchwork filter is heavily reliant on the source image. The filter, like Extrude (see pages 396–397), extrudes squares from the image. In the case of Patchwork, lighter squares are "raised up," while darker ones "pushed back." However, with only two levels of control with which to experiment, the filter's creative boundaries are quickly exhausted.

ORIGINAL IMAGE

DEFAULT PATCHWORK
This bright, colorful image, with very few tonally flat areas, lends itself well to the Patchwork filter.

Settings
Square Size 4
Relief 8

MOSAIC
With maximum Square Size and no extrusion due to a Relief setting of 0, the filter creates a soft, highly pixelated image—in many ways producing a more convincing mosaic than the Mosaic filter (see pages 380–381)—with each tile. The Square Size is affected by the image's resolution.

Settings
Square Size 10
Relief 0

DEFAULT

Patchwork	⇕
Square Size	4
Relief	8

FILTER SETTING PARAMETERS

Square Size	Min **0**	Max **10**
Relief	Min **0**	Max **25**

ORIGINAL IMAGE

Settings
Square Size 10
Relief 25

Settings
Square Size 8
Relief 7

SQUARES

In areas sharing similar tones—like the sky in this shot—the filter has nothing much to work on and can only produce rows of regular squares. Even with a variety of settings ranging from maximum (above) to more conservative values (left), the results are somewhat predictable.

ORIGINAL IMAGE

TEXTURE AND DETAIL

Returning to the more tonally random natural world instantly produces results with some artistic merit. Experimenting with both controls in tandem determines how much or how little texture and detail is retained.

With low Square Size and high Relief, texture and detail are at their most apparent.

Settings
Square Size 3
Relief 24

Reversing the controls creates a more blocky, pixelated result.

Settings
Square Size 9
Relief 7

PATCHWORK

DEFAULT

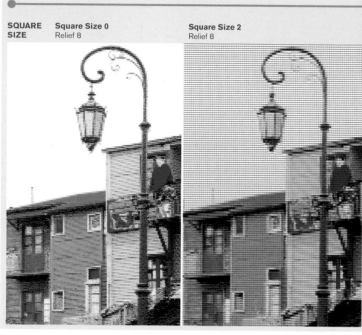

SQUARE SIZE

Square Size 0
Relief 8

Square Size 2
Relief 8

Square Size 4
Relief 4

Square Size 4
Relief 16

Square Size 4
Relief 25

DEFAULT

FILTER SETTING PARAMETERS

Square Size	Min	**0**	Max	**10**
Relief	Min	**0**	Max	**25**

Square Size 7
Relief 8

Square Size 10
Relief 8

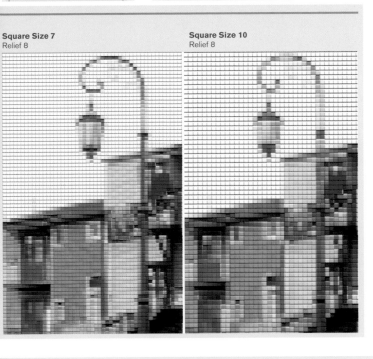

RELIEF

Square Size 4
Relief 0

MIXED SETTINGS

Square Size 0
Relief 1

Square Size 1
Relief 25

Square Size 10
Relief 12

INTRODUCING STAINED GLASS

The Stained Glass filter divides an image into a random pattern of irregularly shaped cells. Each cell is uniform in tone and color—which is determined by the values of the corresponding pixels in the unfiltered image—and separated from its neighbor by a distinctive dividing line, the color of which is determined by the Foreground Color selection.

ORIGINAL IMAGE

DEFAULT STAINED GLASS
The size of the cells is determined by the image's resolution. With this low-resolution 2 MB file, the cell size is appropriate for the image.

Settings
Cell Size 10
Border Thickness 4
Light Intensity 3

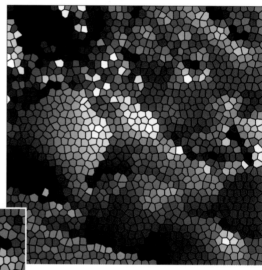

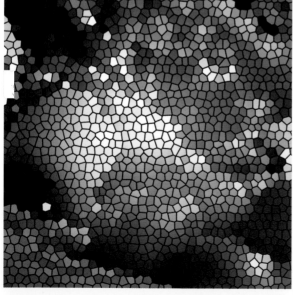

LIGHT
Increasing the Light Intensity setting is intended to replicate sunlight shining through the window.

Settings
Cell Size 10
Border Thickness 4
Light Intensity 7

Foreground/
Background
Colors

DEFAULT

Stained Glass	
Cell Size	10
Border Thickness	4
Light Intensity	3

FILTER SETTING PARAMETERS

Cell Size	Min **2**	Max **50**
Border Thickness	Min **1**	Max **20**
Light Intensity	Min **0**	Max **10**

ORIGINAL IMAGE

HONEYCOMB

With near minimum settings for the Cell Size and Border Thickness, a honeycomb effect is the result.

Settings
Cell Size 3
Border Thickness 1
Light Intensity 3

WHITE BORDER

Inverting the Foreground and Background Colors (press x), the cell borders become the white Foreground Color.

Settings
Cell Size 3
Border Thickness 1
Light Intensity 3

Foreground/
Background
Colors

ORIGINAL IMAGE

ABSTRACT

Experimenting with different Foreground Colors and increasing the Cell Size to beyond the reality of stained glass can produce some pleasing colorful abstracts.

Foreground/
Background
Colors

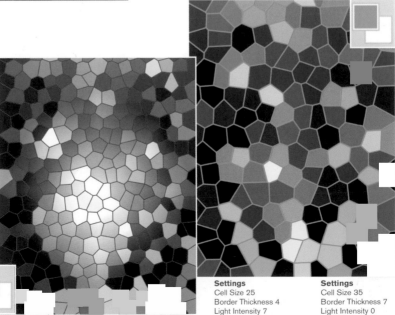

Settings
Cell Size 25
Border Thickness 4
Light Intensity 7

Settings
Cell Size 35
Border Thickness 7
Light Intensity 0

STAINED GLASS

DEFAULT

CELL SIZE

Cell Size 2
Border Thickness 4
Light Intensity 3

Cell Size 6
Border Thickness 4
Light Intensity 3

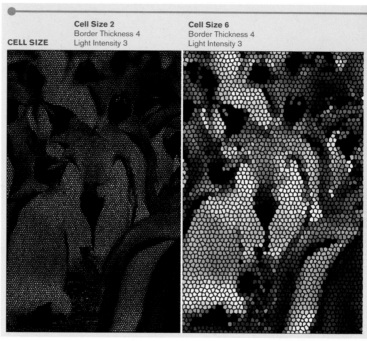

Cell Size 10
Border Thickness 9
Light Intensity 3

Cell Size 10
Border Thickness 18
Light Intensity 3

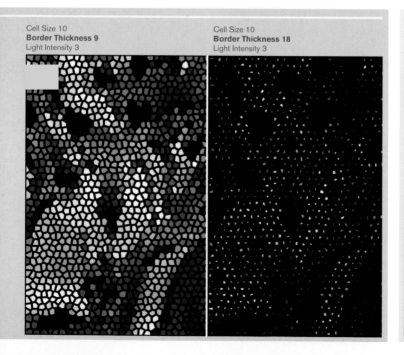

LIGHT INTENSITY

Cell Size 10
Border Thickness 4
Light Intensity 10

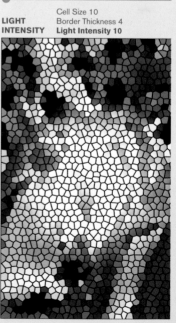

DEFAULT

Stained Glass

Cell Size	10
Border Thickness	4
Light Intensity	3

FILTER SETTING PARAMETERS

Cell Size	Min **2**	Max **50**
Border Thickness	Min **1**	Max **20**
Light Intensity	Min **0**	Max **10**

Cell Size 15
Border Thickness 4
Light Intensity 3

Cell Size 46
Border Thickness 4
Light Intensity 3

BORDER THICKNESS Cell Size 10
Border Thickness 1
Light Intensity 3

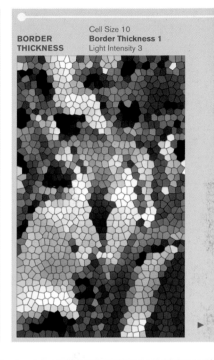

MIXED SETTINGS
Cell Size 3
Border Thickness 1
Light Intensity 0

Cell Size 7
Border Thickness 2
Light Intensity 10

Cell Size 17
Border Thickness 15
Light Intensity 0

INTRODUCING TEXTURIZER

Texturizer uses the same options—Brick, Burlap, Canvas, and Sandstone—as Conté Crayon, Rough Pastels, and Underpainting, but unlike those other filters, Texturizer only has controls that affect the selected texture—the image itself remains untouched. As with other Photoshop filters, Texturizer is probably most successfully used in tandem with another.

ORIGINAL IMAGE

DEFAULT TEXURIZER
Canvas is the default Texture option, and it successfully recreates the look of roughly textured art canvas; although careful observation reveals a repeat pattern at this scale with this three-megapixel image.

Settings
Texture: Canvas
Scaling 100%
Relief 4
Light: Top

SANDSTONE
The Sandstone Texture produces a more random, art paper look. With this setting at more or less standard Scaling and Relief, the light direction makes little difference.

Settings
Texture: Sandstone
Scaling 123%
Relief 11
Light: Left

DEFAULT

FILTER SETTING PARAMETERS

Scaling	Min **50%**	Max **200%**
Relief	Min **0**	Max **50**

BRICK
Texturizer's Brick option places a convincing brick shape and texture over the image. Relief settings need to remain low for the image to remain legible.

Settings
Texture: Brick
Scaling 196%
Relief 7
Light: Top Right

ORIGINAL IMAGE

HIGH RELIEF
Increasing the Relief setting increases the contrast of the texture, so rendering the image harder to read.

Settings
Texture: Brick
Scaling 196%
Relief 33
Light: Top Right

ORIGINAL IMAGE

☐ Invert

☑ Invert

INVERSION
Found beneath the Light option is a small check box labeled Invert. Although the effect is subtle, with the exaggerated settings used here it's possible to see how Invert reverses the texture, so that elements that were recessed become raised, and vice versa.

Settings (for both images)
Texture: Burlap
Scaling 169%
Relief 6
Light: Top Left

TEXTURIZER
BRICK

DEFAULT BRICK TEXTURE

SCALING   **Scaling 50%**   **Scaling 150%**
Relief 4   Relief 4

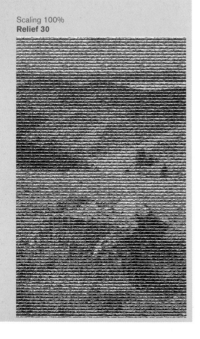

Scaling 100%
Relief 30

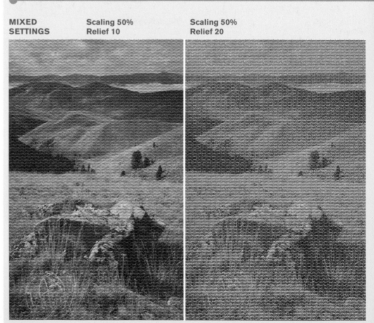

MIXED   **Scaling 50%**   **Scaling 50%**
SETTINGS   **Relief 10**   **Relief 20**

DEFAULT

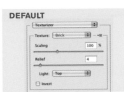

FILTER SETTING PARAMETERS

Scaling	Min **50%**	Max **200%**
Relief	Min **0**	Max **50**

Scaling 200%
Relief 4

RELIEF

Scaling 100%
Relief 10

Scaling 100%
Relief 20

Scaling 150%
Relief 12

Scaling 200%
Relief 8

Scaling 200%
Relief 15

TEXTURIZER
BURLAP

DEFAULT BURLAP TEXTURE

SCALING   Scaling 50%   Scaling 150%
Relief 4   Relief 4

Scaling 100%
Relief 30

MIXED SETTINGS   Scaling 50%   Scaling 50%
Relief 10   Relief 20

DEFAULT

Scaling	Min **50%**	Max **200%**
Relief	Min **0**	Max **50**

Scaling 200%
Relief 4

RELIEF   Scaling 100%
Relief 10   Scaling 100%
Relief 20

Scaling 150%
Relief 12

Scaling 200%
Relief 8

Scaling 200%
Relief 15

TEXTURIZER
SANDSTONE

DEFAULT SANDSTONE TEXTURE

SCALING

Scaling 50%
Relief 4

Scaling 150%
Relief 4

Scaling 100%
Relief 30

MIXED SETTINGS

Scaling 50%
Relief 10

Scaling 50%
Relief 20

DEFAULT

FILTER SETTING PARAMETERS

Scaling	Min **50%**	Max **200%**
Relief	Min **0**	Max **50**

Scaling 200%
Relief 4

RELIEF

Scaling 100%
Relief 10

Scaling 100%
Relief 20

▶

Scaling 150%
Relief 12

Scaling 200%
Relief 8

Scaling 200%
Relief 15

COMBINING FILTERS

Here is a taste of the myriad of different effects you can achieve by combining filters in the Filter Gallery. Here only two filters are used together, but there is nothing to prevent you from adding more and working with multiple filters. For instructions on how to build up filter effects in the Filter Gallery, see pages 18–19.

COMBINING FILTERS

Foreground/
Background
Colors

ANGLED STROKES
Direction Balance 50
Stroke Length 15
Sharpness 3

MOSAIC TILES
Tile Size 12
Grout Width 3
Lighten Grout 9

Foreground/
Background
Colors

DIFFUSE GLOW
Graininess 5
Glow Amount 3
Clear Amount 20

FILM GRAIN
Grain 4
Highlight Area 13
Intensity 10

Foreground/
Background
Colors

PHOTOCOPY
Detail 8
Darkness 14

CUTOUT
Number of Levels 8
Edge Simplicity 0
Edge Fidelity 1

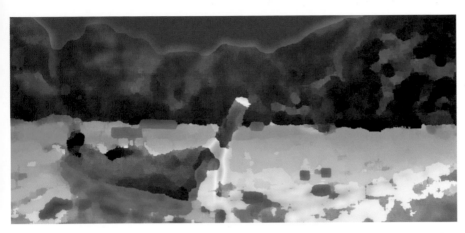

Foreground/
Background
Colors

PALETTE KNIFE
Stroke Size 25
Stroke Detail 3
Softness 0

COLORED PENCIL
Pencil Width 5
Stroke Pressure 9
Paper Brightness 25

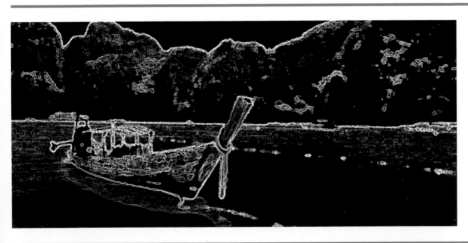

GLOWING EDGES
Edge Width 1
Edge Brightness 15
Smoothness 3

WATER PAPER
Fiber Length 9
Brightness 53
Contrast 81

INK OUTLINES
Stroke Length 4
Dark Intensity 20
Light Intensity 10

POSTER EDGES
Edge Thickness 2
Edge Intensity 1
Posterization 2

COMBINING FILTERS

CROSSHATCH
Stroke Length 9
Sharpness 6
Strength 1

GLASS
Distortion 5
Smoothness 3
Texture: Frosted
Scaling 100%

PAINT DAUBS
Brush Size 8
Sharpness 7
Brush Type: Wide Blurry

SMUDGE STICK
Stroke Length 2
Highlight Area 0
Intensity 10

Foreground/
Background
Colors

WATERCOLOR
Brush Detail 9
Shadow Intensity 1
Texture 1

CHALK & CHARCOAL
Charcoal Area 6
Chalk Area 6
Stroke Pressure 1

Foreground/
Background Colors

STAINED GLASS
Cell Size 2
Border Thickness 1
Light Intensity 3

ROUGH PASTELS
Stroke Length 6
Stroke Detail 4
Texture: Canvas
Scaling 100%
Relief 20
Light: Bottom

Foreground/
Background
Colors

FRESCO
Brush Size 3
Brush Detail 3
Texture 3

GRAPHIC PEN
Stroke Length 4
Light/Dark Balance 60
Stroke Direction:
Right Diagonal

SPRAYED STROKES
Stroke Length 12
Spray Radius 7
Stroke Direction:
Right Diagonal

TEXTURIZER
Texture: Burlap
Scaling 100%
Relief 4
Light: Top

COMBINING FILTERS

DRY BRUSH
Brush Size 0
Brush Detail 10
Texture 3

SMUDGE STICK
Stroke Length 0
Highlight Area 8
Intensity 10

NOTE PAPER
Image Balance 24
Graininess 0
Relief 2

NEON GLOW
Glow Size 5
Glow Brightness 15

SPONGE
Brush Size 2
Definition 12
Smoothness 5

ACCENTED EDGES
Edge Width 2
Edge Brightness 38
Smoothness 5

SPATTER
Spray Radius 5
Smoothness 4

PATCHWORK
Square Size 1
Relief 2

DARK STROKES
Balance 8
Black Intensity 1
White Intensity 5

PLASTIC WRAP
Highlight Strength 2
Detail 15
Smoothness 9

CRAQUELURE
Crack Spacing 28
Crack Depth 2
Crack Brightness 4

UNDERPAINTING
Brush Size 0
Texture Coverage 7
Texture: Sandstone
Scaling 100%
Relief 4
Light: Top

THE SCOPE OF FILTERS

Like the previous section Combining Filters, this short section is a taster, giving you an idea about how you can modify your image once you've applied one or two filters, mostly by using the Fade command and by blending layers together. The methods explored here are by no means comprehensive—as you become

familiar with working with filters in Photoshop, you should develop a sense of how extensive the possibilities are. For instructions on how to use the Fade command and layer blending features, see page 20.

COLORED PENCIL

By fading the filter after applying it, you can reduce the impact on the image and apply different blending modes to create different effects. Here, the Colored Pencil filter is applied with two Fade effects.

ORIGINAL IMAGE

COLORED PENCIL

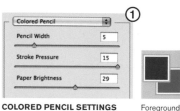

COLORED PENCIL SETTINGS

Foreground/Background Colors

1. Once you've applied the Colored Pencil filter with the settings above using the Foreground/Background Colors as shown, go to Edit > Fade Colored Pencil.

Edit	Image	Layer	Select	Filte
Undo Colored Pencil				⌘Z
Step Forward				⇧⌘Z
Step Backward				⌥⌘Z
Fade Colored Pencil...				⇧⌘F
Cut				⌘X

2. The Fade dialog box appears, and you can apply the settings as indicated below left.

COLORED PENCIL AND FADE WITH DIFFERENCE MODE

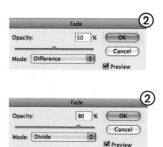

COLORED PENCIL AND FADE WITH DIVIDE MODE

CUTOUT

The Cutout filter can give an image a vivid illustrative look with brightened sharp colors.

ORIGINAL IMAGE

CUTOUT

1. Duplicate the Background layer by dragging the layer down to the Create a new layer icon at the bottom of the Layers palette.
2. Turn the new layer into a Smart Layer by selecting it and going to Filter > Convert for Smart Filters. This enables you to adjust the filter settings later if you want to.

3. To apply the Cutout filter, go to Filter > Artistic > Cutout. Here we used the settings below.

CUTOUT SETTINGS

4. Finally, change the blending mode to Overlay.

CUTOUT WITH OVERLAY MODE

DRY BRUSH

When applied on its own, the Dry Brush filter creates a variety of painterly effects; however, these can be further enhanced by experimenting with any of the blending modes.

ORIGINAL IMAGE

DRY BRUSH

DRY BRUSH SETTINGS

1. Apply the Dry Brush filter to the image with the settings shown above.
2. Go to Edit > Fade Dry Brush. In the Fade dialog box, set Mode to Darken.

The Dry Brush effect is lessened by fading it using the Darken blending mode, which allows more of the original image to show.

The image on the right had the Dry Brush filter applied twice (both with the same settings as shown above).
3. Once you've applied the Dry Brush filter, go to Edit > Fade Dry Brush. In the Fade dialog box, experiment with various Opacity and blending mode options. Here, we've used 25% Opacity and set Mode to Hard Mix.

A stronger result from applying the filter twice but fading the second application with the settings shown below.

FILM GRAIN

Initially, the Film Grain filter is applied strongly, but it creates a delicate painterly picture once the blending mode and Opacity of the duplicated layer have been adjusted.

ORIGINAL IMAGE

FILM GRAIN

FILM GRAIN SETTINGS

1. Duplicate the Background layer by dragging it down to the Create a new layer icon at the bottom of the Layers palette.
2. Turn the new layer into a Smart Layer by selecting it and going to Filter > Convert for Smart Filters.

3. Apply the Film Grain filter to the copied layer by going to Filter > Artistic > Film Grain. Here we used the settings shown above right.

4. To create a more delicate effect, change the blending mode to Luminosity and adjust the Opacity to 60%.

FINAL FILM GRAIN EFFECT

FRESCO

Here, the original image is again blended with the copied layer that's had the Fresco filter applied. Reducing the Opacity makes the effect a little less stark.

ORIGINAL IMAGE

FRESCO

FRESCO SETTINGS

1. Duplicate the Background layer by dragging it down to the Create a new layer icon at the bottom of the Layers palette.
2. Turn the new layer into a Smart Layer by selecting it and going to Filter > Convert for Smart Filters.
3. Apply the Fresco filter to the copied layer by going to Filter > Artistic > Fresco. Here, the settings above right were used.
4. You can then play with the blending modes and Opacity. The top image has Vivid Light blending mode with an Opacity of 50%; the bottom image has a Subtract blending mode and an Opacity of 30%.

The Fresco filter applied to the second layer, with the blending mode changed to Vivid Light and Opacity reduced to 50%, creates a brighter, more colorful result than the original.

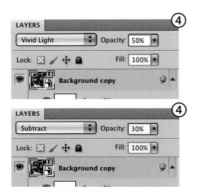

The Subtract blending mode was selected with an Opacity of 30% to produce this stormy looking effect.

PAINT DAUBS

By applying the Paint Daubs filter and then fading it with the Divide blending mode, you can create the look of a line-drawn illustration.

ORIGINAL IMAGE

PAINT DAUBS

PAINT DAUBS SETTINGS

1. In this example, the Paint Daubs filter is applied to the Background without converting it for Smart Filters. Go to Filter > Artistic > Paint Daubs and apply the settings indicated above right.

2. Once you have applied the filter, go to Edit > Fade Paint Daubs and select Divide from the Mode drop-down menu. Click OK.
3. At the bottom of the Layers palette, click the Create new fill or adjustment layer button and select

Curves. Adjust the curve by clicking and dragging the point as shown to darken the image.
4. You can change the curve again by double-clicking the Curves adjustment layer that appears in the Layers palette.

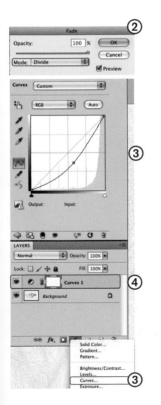

Here, the Paint Daubs filter was applied, faded with the Divide blending mode, and finished with a Curves adjustment layer.

PALETTE KNIFE AND POSTER EDGES

Here, two filters are combined by applying them to the duplicated image on separate layers and changing the blending mode and Opacity between them.

ORIGINAL IMAGE

PALETTE KNIFE

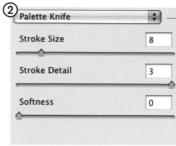

PALETTE KNIFE SETTINGS

1. Duplicate the original image by dragging the Background layer down to the Create a new layer icon at the bottom of the Layers palette.
2. Select the Background layer and go to Filter > Artistic > Palette Knife. Apply the settings shown above right and click OK. (You won't see any difference because the new Background copy layer above now hides the original Background layer.)
3. Select the Background copy layer and go to Filter > Artistic > Poster Edges. Apply the settings shown right and click OK.
4. You can change the blending mode and Opacity. Here, Overlay Blend Mode is applied with an Opacity of 50%.

POSTER EDGES

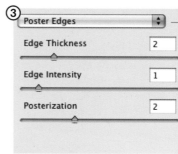

POSTER EDGES SETTINGS

The Poster Edges filter is blended with the Palette Knife filter using Overlay set at an Opacity of 50% to produce this painterly image.

NEON GLOW AND PLASTIC WRAP

Both Neon Glow and Plastic Wrap are powerful Artistic filters; however, with sympathetic color selection and careful use of blending modes they can work together with creative surreal results.

ORIGINAL IMAGE

Foreground/
Background
Colors

NEON GLOW SETTINGS

Neon Glow	
Glow Size	-10
Glow Brightness	39
Glow Color	

PLASTIC WRAP SETTINGS

Plastic Wrap	
Highlight Strength	17
Detail	4
Smoothness	11

1. Duplicate the Background layer by dragging it down to the Create a new layer icon at the bottom of the Layers palette.
2. Taking each layer in turn, go to Filter > Convert for Smart Filters so you can adjust the settings later if desired.

3. Set Foreground/Background Colors as shown. These colors are sourced from the original image. Select the bottom layer (now called Layer 2) and go to Filter > Artistic > Neon Glow. Use the settings as shown above and click OK. (You won't see any difference on the image because the Background copy layer hides the Layer 2 layer.)

4. Select the Background copy layer and go to Filter > Artistic > Plastic Wrap. Apply the settings shown above right and click OK.
5. With the Background copy still selected, play around with the different blending mode options. Here, Linear Light was selected and an Opacity of 75%.

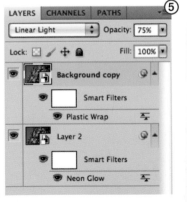

This is the result of blending the Plastic Wrap and Neon Glow filters using the Linear Light blending mode and an Opacity of 75%.

ROUGH PASTELS

An extreme pastel illustration results by applying the Rough Pastels filter to both the original Background layer and a duplicated layer, with Screen blending mode used to lighten the whole effect.

ORIGINAL IMAGE

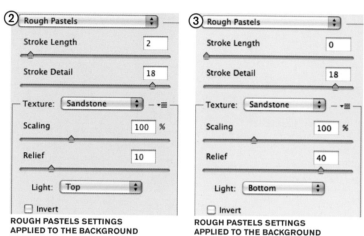

ROUGH PASTELS SETTINGS APPLIED TO THE BACKGROUND LAYER

ROUGH PASTELS SETTINGS APPLIED TO THE BACKGROUND COPY LAYER

1. Duplicate the original image by dragging the Background layer down to the Create a new layer icon in the Layers palette.
2. Select the Background layer and go to Filter > Artistic > Rough Pastels. For this image, the settings above left were applied. Click OK. (You won't see any difference because the new Background copy layer above hides the original Background.)
3. Select the Background copy layer and go to Filter > Artistic > Rough Pastels. Apply the settings shown above right and click OK.
4. To create a lighter, pastel effect, change the Background copy layer's blending mode to Screen in the Layers palette and set an Opacity of 50%.

By blending two layers that have Rough Pastels applied with different settings, this lighter, more pastel-like effect is generated.

SMUDGE STICK

This photograph is changed from a soft gentle dusk to a moody, darker, more intense picture by using the Smudge Stick filter and the Fade command with Linear Burn blending mode.

ORIGINAL IMAGE

SMUDGE STICK

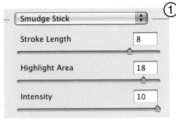

SMUDGE STICK SETTINGS

1. Apply the Smudge Stick filter by going to Filter > Artistic > Smudge Stick and using the settings above right. It creates a strong effect, as you can see in the image above right.
2. Go to Edit > Fade Smudge Stick and the dialog box below appears.
3. Change Mode to Linear Burn and Opacity to 40%.

To create this more intense look, a high value for the Highlight Area and Intensity was used with the Smudge Stick filter, and then faded using Linear Burn blending mode at 40% Opacity.

SPONGE AND UNDERPAINTING

There are many different effects that can be achieved using this combination of filters applied to two separate layers. This one gives an etched effect.

ORIGINAL IMAGE

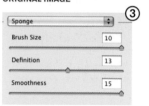

SPONGE SETTINGS

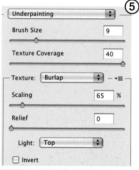

UNDERPAINTING SETTINGS

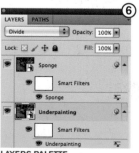

LAYERS PALETTE

1. To apply the filters to two separate layers, duplicate the Background layer twice by dragging it down to the Create a new layer icon at the bottom of the Layers palette.
2. With each layer, go to Filter > Convert for Smart Filters so you can adjust the settings later if you want to.
3. Select the Sponge layer and go to Filter > Artistic > Sponge. For this image, the settings to the left were applied.

4. Apply the Subtract blending mode to the Sponge layer.
5. Select the Underpainting Layer and go to Filter > Artistic > Underpainting. The settings middle left were used here.
6. Apply the Divide blending mode to the Underpainting layer.

The Sponge and Underpainting filters applied to two duplicate layers creates a color wash and color shift effect.

WATERCOLOR

This is an interesting effect using the Watercolor filter applied to two layers, with the Dissolve blending mode set at 70% Opacity bringing texture to the image.

ORIGINAL IMAGE

WATERCOLOR SETTINGS FOR THE TOP LAYER

WATERCOLOR SETTINGS FOR THE MIDDLE LAYER

1. To apply the filters to two separate layers, duplicate the Background layer twice by dragging it down to the Create a new layer icon at the bottom of the Layers palette.
2. Select each of the Layers one at a time and go to Filter > Convert for Smart Filters.

3. Select the top Background copy and go to Filter > Artistic > Watercolor and apply the settings on the left above.
4. Change the blending mode to Dissolve and Opacity to 60%.
5. Select Background copy 2 below, go to Filter > Artistic > Watercolor, and apply the settings in the top right.

6. Change the blending mode of the layer to Overlay and the Opacity to 70%.
7. You can adjust the settings for each of the Watercolor layers by double-clicking the Smart Filters text.

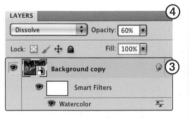

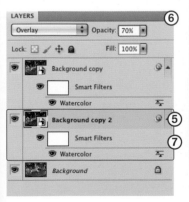

The final image, which can be adjusted by changing the filter settings, blending modes, and Opacity of each of the layers.

ACCENTED EDGES AND CROSSHATCH

Accented Edges draws out the Crosshatch effect, maintaining more detail in combination than would otherwise be the case.

ORIGINAL IMAGE

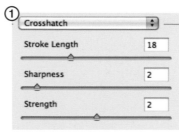

CROSSHATCH SETTINGS

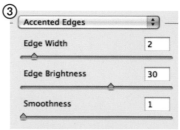

ACCENTED EDGES SETTINGS

1. Apply the Crosshatch filter to the Background. Go to Filter > Brush Strokes > Crosshatch and apply the settings shown above left.
2. Duplicate the Background by dragging it down to the Create a new layer icon at the bottom of the Layers palette.

3. Apply the Accented Edges filter to the duplicated layer using the settings shown above right.
4. Change the Opacity of the top layer to 50%, allowing the Background to show through.

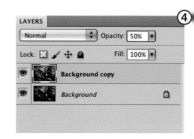

This combination of Crosshatch and Accented Edges filters gives a color-enhanced, ink drawing effect.

DARK STROKES

This use of the Dark Strokes filter is useful if you want to intensify the contrast and saturation of colors in an image.

ORIGINAL IMAGE

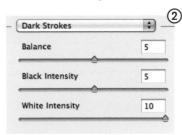

DARK STROKES SETTINGS

1. Duplicate the Background layer by dragging it down to the Create a new layer icon at the bottom of the Layers palette.
2. Select the Background copy layer and go to Filter > Brush Strokes > Dark Strokes. Apply the settings above and click OK.

3. Then go to Edit > Fade Dark Strokes. Change the blending mode to Color Dodge and click OK.
4. Change the blending mode of the Background copy layer to Vivid Light and set the Opacity to 70%.

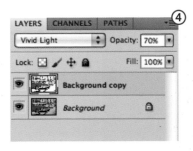

With the Dark Strokes filter applied with some creative blending modes, a bright, and in places burned out, vividly colored image results.

SPRAYED STROKES AND DIFFUSE GLOW

Using the Sprayed Strokes filter on two separate layers, with strokes going in opposite directions, creates a crosshatch effect that combines with Diffuse Glow to create this powerfully illustrative result.

ORIGINAL IMAGE

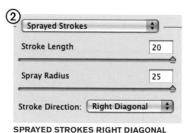

SPRAYED STROKES RIGHT DIAGONAL

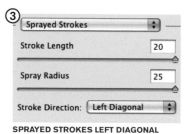

SPRAYED STROKES LEFT DIAGONAL

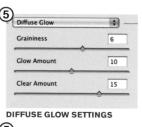

DIFFUSE GLOW SETTINGS

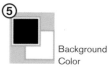

Background Color

1. Duplicate the Background layer three times by dragging it down to the Create a new layer icon in the Layers palette.
2. Select the next layer up from the Background layer and go to Filter > Brush Strokes > Sprayed Strokes. Apply the settings shown above left using Right Diagonal Stroke Direction.
3. Select the next layer up and again go to Filter > Brush Strokes > Sprayed Strokes. Use the settings shown above right, with Left Diagonal Stroke Direction.
4. Change the Opacity of the layer to 50%. You won't notice any change because the top layer still covers the layers below.
5. Select the top layer and go to Filter > Distort > Diffuse Glow. Apply the settings shown above middle and click OK. In this image, the Background Color (which controls the glow color) is white.
6. Now change the Blend Mode for this layer to Overlay and the Opacity to 50%.

Two Sprayed Strokes layers add crosshatch texture to this image while the Diffuse Glow layer with the Overlay blending mode boosts the color and highlights.

OCEAN RIPPLE AND BAS RELIEF

Ocean Ripple and Bas Relief both introduce texture to the surface of the image, albeit in very different ways. The result is a textured, out of register color effect.

ORIGINAL IMAGE

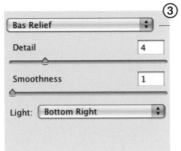

BAS RELIEF SETTINGS

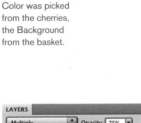

The Foreground Color was picked from the cherries, the Background from the basket.

1. Create two copies of the Background layer by dragging it down to the Create a new layer icon in the Layers palette.

2. Select each of the new layers in turn and go to Filter > Convert for Smart Filters.

3. Before you apply the Bas Relief filter, select the Foreground/Background Colors you want to use for the filter. Select the middle layer, go to Filter > Sketch > Bas Relief, and apply the settings top right.

4. With the layer still selected, apply the Vivid Light blending mode and change the Opacity to 60%.

5. Select the top layer, go to Filter > Distort > Ocean Ripple, and apply the settings shown above middle.

6. With the layer selected, change the blending mode to Multiply and the Opacity to 75%.

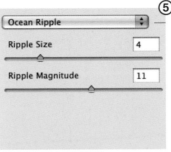

OCEAN RIPPLE SETTINGS

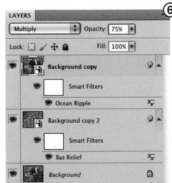

A textured, color-shifted image results from the application of both Ocean Ripple and Bas Relief filters.

CHALK & CHARCOAL

This is a simple effect where the Chalk & Charcoal filter is applied to a duplicate layer, while a reduced Opacity allows more color to shine through from the layer below.

ORIGINAL IMAGE

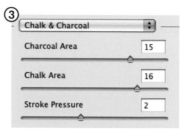

CHALK & CHARCOAL SETTINGS

1. Duplicate the Background layer by dragging it down to the Create a new layer icon at the bottom of the Layers palette.
2. Go to Filter > Convert for Smart Filters so that you can adjust the Filter settings later.

3. With the Background copy layer selected, go to Filter > Sketch > Chalk & Charcoal and apply the settings above.
4. Reduce the Opacity of the Background copy layer to 60% or until the colors from the Background layer show through to the extent you want.

Using an Opacity of 75% while leaving the Blend Mode as Normal subtly adjusts the Chalk & Charcoal effect.

CHROME

It's usually difficult to decipher the original image after applying the Chrome filter, but using the Divide blending mode can create some interesting effects that overlay the original image instead.

ORIGINAL IMAGE

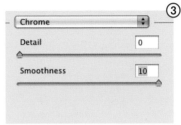

CHROME SETTINGS

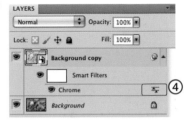

1. Duplicate the Background layer by dragging it down to the Create a new layer icon at the bottom of the Layers palette.
2. Go to Filter > Convert to Smart Filters so that you can change the settings you like afterward.

3. With the layer still selected, go to Filter > Sketch > Chrome and apply the settings shown above.
4. To reintroduce some color, double-click the Chrome blending options icon in the Layers palette, and in the Blending Options dialog box select Divide and set Opacity to 65%.

This interesting texture and color arises from reducing the effect of the Chrome filter by adjusting the Blending Options of the Smart Filter layer.

CONTÉ CRAYON

You can use the color wash and texture that is applied with the Conté Crayon to add intensity to an image.

ORIGINAL IMAGE

 ③

Foreground/
Background Colors

1. Duplicate the Background layer by dragging it down to the Create a new layer icon at the bottom of the Layers palette.
2. Go to Filter > Convert for Smart Filters.
3. Before you apply the Conté Crayon filter, choose a Foreground and Background Color. For this example, colors were taken from the image.

4. With the layer selected, go to Filter > Sketch > Conté Crayon and apply the settings shown middle left.
5. Change the Background copy layer's blending mode to Exclusion and Opacity to 70%.

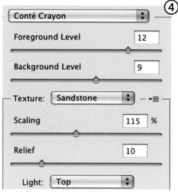 ④

CONTÉ CRAYON SETTINGS

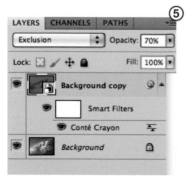 ⑤

Blending the Conté Crayon filter layer in with the original image applies a color wash. The texture is also visible and could be adjusted by changing the filter settings again.

NOTE PAPER

Some unexpected color shifts can be created by blending a layer that has had the Note Paper filter applied with the original image.

ORIGINAL IMAGE

Foreground/
Background Colors

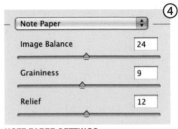

NOTE PAPER SETTINGS

1. Duplicate the Background layer by dragging it down to the Create a new layer icon at the bottom of the Layers palette.
2. Go to Filter > Convert to Smart Filters so that you can change the settings afterward.
3. Before you apply the Note Paper filter, set Foreground/ Background Colors to those shown here.

4. With the Background copy layer still selected, go to Filter > Sketch > Note Paper and apply the settings shown above.
5. With the layer selected, change the blending mode to Darken and Opacity to 50%.

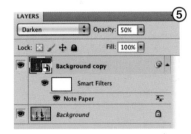

Pictures with simple shapes work best with the Note Paper filter, which creates textured blocks that here blend in with the original image.

PHOTOCOPY AND RETICULATION

Combining these two filters creates some strong and unusual textures.
You can vary the blending modes to give more subtle or stronger color shifts.

ORIGINAL IMAGE

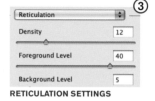

③

RETICULATION SETTINGS

Reticulation	
Density	12
Foreground Level	40
Background Level	5

⑤

Foreground/
Background
Colors used
for the
Photocopy filter.

⑤

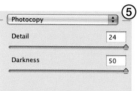

PHOTOCOPY SETTINGS

Photocopy	
Detail	24
Darkness	50

1. To create two duplicate layers, drag the Background layer down to the Create a new layer icon at the bottom of the Layers palette.
2. Select each new layer in turn and go to Filter > Convert for Smart Filters.

3. Select the middle Layer and go to Filter > Sketch > Reticulation and apply the settings shown above left.
4. With the layer still selected, change the blending mode to Overlay and Opacity to 40%.

5. Select the top layer and go to Filter > Sketch > Photocopy and apply the settings shown above right. For this image, Foreground and Background Colors were selected from within the image.
6. With the top layer still selected, change the blending mode to Overlay and Opacity to 60%.

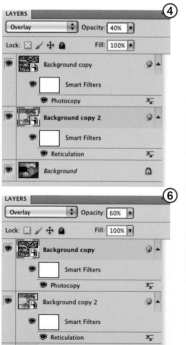

The Photocopy and Reticulation filters were applied to separate layers, and both have the Overlay blending mode applied along with reduced Opacity.

TORN EDGES AND GLOWING EDGES

You can dim the Glowing Edges filter by blending it with the original layer and by adding a layer on top that has had the Torn Edges filter applied.

ORIGINAL IMAGE

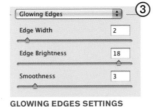 ③

Glowing Edges

Edge Width	2
Edge Brightness	18
Smoothness	3

GLOWING EDGES SETTINGS

 ⑤

Foreground/
Background
Colors used
for the Torn
Edges filter.

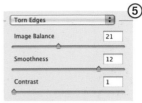 ⑤

Torn Edges

Image Balance	21
Smoothness	12
Contrast	1

TORN EDGES SETTINGS

1. Duplicate the Background layer twice by dragging it down to the Create a new layer icon at the bottom of the Layers palette.
2. Select each new layer in turn and go to Filter > Convert for Smart Filters.

3. Select the middle Layer, go to Filter > Stylize > Glowing Edges, and apply the settings shown above left.
4. With the layer still selected, change the blending mode to Divide and Opacity to 75%.

5. Select the top layer and go to Filter > Sketch > Torn Edges and apply the settings shown above right. For this image, Foreground and Background Colors were selected from within the image.
6. With the layer still selected, change the blending mode to Overlay and Opacity to 50%.

Both the Torn Edges and the Glowing Edges filters have been applied and blended with the original image to create a vivid, glowing illustrative effect.

HALFTONE PATTERN

By applying the Halftone Pattern filter and then fading it by applying the Difference blending mode, some interesting color shifts and textures appear in the image.

1. With the Background layer selected go to Filter > Convert for Smart Filters so that you can change the settings if you want later.

2. Go to Filter > Sketch > Halftone Pattern and apply the settings shown below. You can see the effect the filter has on the image below.

3. Go to Edit > Fade Halftone Pattern and the Fade dialog box appears.

4. Select Difference as the Mode and click OK to produce the final image, shown below right.

ORIGINAL IMAGE

HALFTONE PATTERN

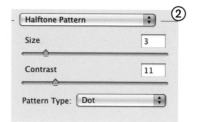

HALFTONE SETTINGS

The final image. The larger size of the Halftone Pattern dot gives an interesting texture.

GRAPHIC PEN AND WATER PAPER

With appropriate Foreground/Background Colors selected, the Graphic Pen filter creates a distinctive two-tone effect, tempered here with the Water Paper filter on a Pin Light blending mode.

1. Duplicate the Background twice by dragging it down to the Create a new layer icon at the bottom of the Layers palette.
2. Select each new Layer in turn and go to Filter > Convert for Smart Filters.
3. With the middle layer selected, set the Foreground and Background Colors from within the image (as shown), go to Filter > Sketch > Graphic Pen, and apply the settings shown right.
4. Select the top layer, go to Filter > Sketch > Water Paper, and apply the settings shown far right.
5. With the top layer still selected, change the blending mode to Pin Light.

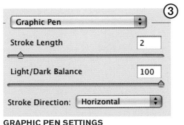

Foreground/ Background Colors used for the Graphic Pen filter.

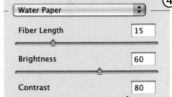

ORIGINAL IMAGE

Graphic Pen	
Stroke Length	2
Light/Dark Balance	100
Stroke Direction:	Horizontal

GRAPHIC PEN SETTINGS

Water Paper	
Fiber Length	15
Brightness	60
Contrast	80

WATER PAPER SETTINGS

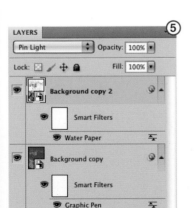

The final image is brightened by the Pin Light blending mode and shows texture from both filters.

STAMP AND CRAQUELURE

Combining these two filters, Stamp and Craquelure, creates some strong and unusual textures. You can vary the blending modes to give more subtle or stronger color shifts as well.

1. Duplicate the Background layer twice by dragging it down to the Create a new layer icon at the bottom of the Layers palette.
2. Select each new layer in turn and go to Filter > Convert for Smart Filters.
3. Select the middle layer and go to Filter > Texture > Craquelure and apply the settings shown above.
4. Select Foreground and Background Colors from within the image.
5. Select the top layer and go to Filter > Sketch > Stamp and apply the settings shown to the right.
6. With the Stamp layer still selected, change the blending mode to Multiply and the Opacity to 70%.

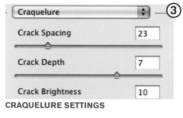

CRAQUELURE SETTINGS

④ Foreground/ Background Colors used for the Stamp filter.

STAMP SETTINGS

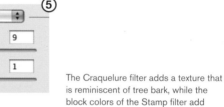

ORIGINAL IMAGE

The Craquelure filter adds a texture that is reminiscent of tree bark, while the block colors of the Stamp filter add an overall sheen.

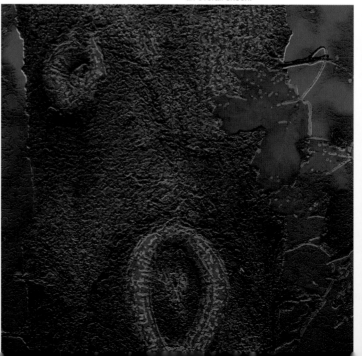

CHARCOAL AND GRAIN

The Grain filter adds a distinctive texture to an image. Here, it's used to overlay the Charcoal filter that gives a "drawn" look to the underlying image.

ORIGINAL IMAGE

Foreground/ Background Colors used for the Charcoal filter.

CHARCOAL SETTINGS

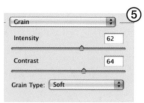

GRAIN SETTINGS

1. Duplicate the Background layer by dragging it down to the Create a new layer icon at the bottom of the Layers palette.
2. Select both layers in turn and go to Filter > Convert for Smart Filters.

3. Select Foreground and Background Colors from within the image.
4. Select the bottom layer and go to Filter > Sketch > Charcoal and apply the settings shown above.

5. Select the top layer and go to Filter > Texture > Grain and apply the settings shown above right.
6. With the top layer still selected, change the blending mode to Color Burn.

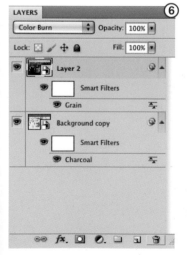

Combining the Grain and Charcoal filters together creates this interesting illustrative-style image.

MOSAIC TILES

Reducing the Tile Size in the Mosaic Tiles settings creates an unexpected texture that has lost the blocky look of tiles. The texture is then blended with the original photograph.

1. Duplicate the layer by dragging the Background down to the Create a new layer icon at the bottom of the Layers palette.
2. Select the duplicate layer and go to Filter > Convert for Smart Filters.
3. With the same layer selected, go to Filter > Texture > Mosaic Tiles and apply the settings shown to the right.
4. With the layer still selected, change the blending mode to Overlay and the Opacity to 50%, or to whatever level you find is appropriate for the strength of texture you want.

ORIGINAL IMAGE

MOSAIC TILES SETTINGS

MOSAIC TILES

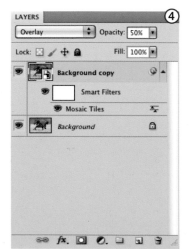

The "tiles" are replaced with this more interesting, less uniform texture that blends well with the underlying image.

PATCHWORK

Here the Patchwork filter was applied with a small Square Size and high Relief, giving an interesting texture to the image.

1. Duplicate the Background layer by dragging it down to the Create a new layer icon at the bottom of the Layers palette.
2. Select the duplicate layer and go to Filter > Convert for Smart Filters.
3. With the same layer selected, go to Filter > Texture > Patchwork and apply the settings shown to the right.
4. With the layer still selected, change the blending mode to Soft Light.

ORIGINAL IMAGE

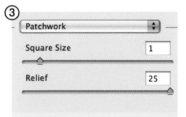

PATCHWORK SETTINGS

PATCHWORK

The Soft Light blending mode blends the Patchwork into the original image.

STAINED GLASS

The Stained Glass filter can leave a picture in a very abstract state. Here, the filter is applied to a duplicate image and then blended with the original, giving a more subtle grid of stained glass.

ORIGINAL IMAGE

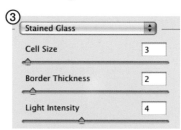

STAINED GLASS SETTINGS

STAINED GLASS

1. Duplicate the Background layer by dragging it down to the Create a new layer icon at the bottom of the Layers palette.
2. Select the duplicate layer and go to Filter > Convert for Smart Filters.

3. With the same layer selected, go to Filter > Texture > Stained Glass and apply the settings shown above.
4. With the layer still selected, change the blending mode to Soft Light.

5. The Soft Light blending mode makes the stained glass effect much more subtle. You can return to the Stained Glass filter settings and increase the size of the Cell and the Border width without the effect overwhelming the picture.

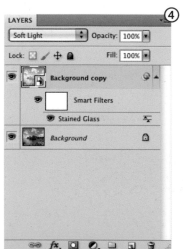

By blending the Stained Glass filter with the original image using the Soft Light blending mode, a subtle grid appears over the image.

TEXTURIZER

The texture added by the Texturizer filter can be a little too strong. This is a simple technique to lessen the impact and create a gentler textured effect.

ORIGINAL IMAGE

TEXTURIZER SETTINGS

TEXTURIZER

1. Duplicate the Background layer by dragging it down to the Create a new layer icon at the bottom of the Layers palette.
2. Select the duplicate layer and go to Filter > Convert for Smart Filters.

3. With the same layer selected, go to Filter > Texture > Texturizer and apply the settings shown above.

4. With the layer still selected, change the Opacity to 50%, or to whatever level you find is appropriate for the strength of texture you want.

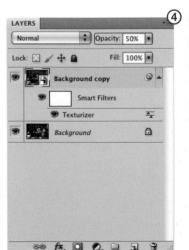

The Burlap texture makes the image look as though it has been printed onto cloth.

OTHER FILTER EFFECTS

Classing these filters as "other" is in no way intended to denigrate their worth. Here you'll find a huge range of filters—many of which Photoshop users could not do without—from the familiar, long-standing Sharpen and Blur filters to filters that are practically applications in themselves, such as the Vanishing Point and Liquify filters.

The filters are presented differently, with the "effects" filters displayed as they are in the Filter Gallery pages and the rest laid out with instructions so that it's clear how to use them.

LENS CORRECTION

The Lens Correction filter offers a selection of camera makes and models and corresponding lenses, and there's a Custom section should you prefer to—or have to—create your own.

ORIGINAL IMAGE

Every camera lens has its own characteristic effect on an image in terms of edge-to-center distortion, vignetting (shading at the corners), and chromatic aberration (scale-distortion of the different RGB color channels toward the extreme edges). With lens profiles that map out these specific flaws, photos can be corrected with a few clicks.

STANDARD CORRECTION

When you open an image in the Lens Correction filter, Photoshop tries to recognize and correct it automatically. If this doesn't happen, select your camera's make, model, and lens type, if available, in the Search Criteria menus. This applies some preset corrections automatically, according to the known characteristics of the lens you choose.

LENS CORRECTION SETTINGS

Geometric Distortion
Auto Scale Image
Camera Make: Nikon Corp.

Lens Profiles
Nikon D90,
Nikon DX 18–200mm
f/3.5-5.6 G ED IF

Don't feel you must stick with the matching lens. These are just presets, so if you're looking for effect rather than technical correction, then browse the different lenses available. You'll find more options if you pick only from the Camera Make menu and jump straight to the Lens Model list.

LENS CORRECTION SETTINGS

Geometric Distortion
Auto Scale Image
Edge: Transparency
Camera Make: Nikon Corp.

Lens Profiles
Nikon D3x,
Nikon FX 16mm f/2.8 D

CHROMATIC ABERRATION

Enable the Chromatic Aberration option in the Correction setting to apply this to the image. This is done according to the presets, so it's important here to use one that matches your actual lens. The Vignette option is also off by default. Enabling this will apply correction for the light fall-off that many lenses produce around the image corners. This is a fairly subtle fix, but it can be very helpful if you want to patch two images together.

ORIGINAL IMAGE

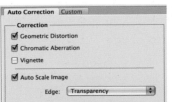

LENS CORRECTION SETTINGS

Geometric Distortion
Chromatic Aberration

Auto Scale Image
Edge: Transparency

AUTO SCALE IMAGE

Some geometric corrections for lenses will scale the image down or up, and gaps may appear around some edges or parts may be cropped off as a result. Turn the Auto Scale Image option on to reclaim parts of the image that are cropped by the geometric correction. Some lenses have noticeable "barrel distortion." If Auto Scale Image is disabled, these corrections will shrink the image. The Edge menu allows you to select from Edge Extension, Transparency (shown here), Black Color, or White Color.

LENS CORRECTION SETTINGS
Geometric Distortion
Lens Profiles
Nikon D90 Sigma DC
18–200mm f3.5–6.3

CUSTOM GEOMETRIC DISTORTION

Use the Custom section to apply your own lens corrections instead of relying on preset lens types. The Geometric Distortion control corrects "pincushion" or barrel distortion created by some lenses. However, you can use this control for artistic effect. Move the slider to the right to introduce "pincushioning," in which the center of the image appears to move away from the viewer, or move the slider to the left to create a barrel effect (see below), in which the center of the scene bulges out toward the viewer.

ORIGINAL IMAGE

LENS CORRECTION SETTINGS
Geometric Distortion
Remove Distortion –60.00

REMOVE DISTORTION TOOL

The Remove Distortion Tool, found in the bar to the left of the image, provides an interactive way of removing (or adding) lens distortion. Click and drag in the image to alter the geometry. Click in the center and drag outward to apply barrel distortion, or click instead in a corner and drag to the center to pull out the edges, applying pincushion distortion.

Remove
Distortion
Tool

LENS CORRECTION SETTINGS
Geometric Distortion
Remove Distortion +100

CUSTOM CHROMATIC ABERRATION

Chromatic aberration is the term for the colored fringes that sometimes appear on contrasting edges of images toward the outer edges. In the Custom panel, use the Red/Cyan Fringe slider to control red and cyan edges, a common problem with some lenses. Other chromatic aberrations can be controlled with the Green/Magenta and Blue/Yellow sliders.

ORIGINAL IMAGE

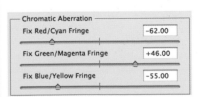

LENS CORRECTION SETTINGS
Chromatic Aberration
Fix Red/Cyan Fringe −62.00
Fix Green/Magenta Fringe +46.00
Fix Blue/Yellow Fringe −55.00

CUSTOM VIGNETTE

Many lenses—particularly today's bundled zoom lenses—produce a certain amount of corner vignetting in photos, whereby the corners are darker than the rest of the image. The Vignette control can be used to correct this. Alternatively, it can be used to introduce a vignette, so encouraging the viewer to focus on the center of the image. The Midpoint slider controls the size of the vignette correction. The Amount slider determines the strength of the filter. The default is 0. Slide the Amount slider to the right to brighten corners, or to the left, as here, to darken them.

ORIGINAL IMAGE

LENS CORRECTION SETTINGS
Vignette
Amount −90

CUSTOM TRANSFORM

The Vertical Perspective slider can be used to correct converging vertical lines of tall buildings, mimicking some of the effects of a tilt-shift lens. In typical cityscape shots, move this slider to the left to make buildings appear straight. The Horizontal Perspective slider uses the same perspective-correcting behavior as Vertical, but turned sideways. The result is like turning the image viewpoint slightly left or right.

LENS CORRECTION SETTINGS
Transform
Vertical Perspective −28

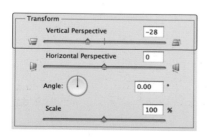

CUSTOM HORIZON CONTROL

The Angle control simply turns the image around a central point, scaling as necessary to avoid creating empty areas in the corners. It's controlled by dragging a line around a circle (fairly difficult to control) or by typing in numbers (easier to control). Use the up and down arrow keys to increment the numbers, and hold down Shift to increment in larger steps.

ORIGINAL IMAGE

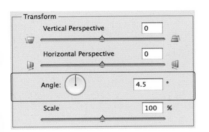

LENS CORRECTION SETTINGS
Transform
Angle: 4.5°

Straighten
Tool

Playing around with a tilted horizon is easiest to do using the Straighten Tool from the toolbar to the left of the image. With this selected, click and drag along a line that should be horizontal. This will apply the necessary rotation angle in the Transform section on the right.

LENS CORRECTION SETTINGS
Transform
Angle: 357.0°

LIQUIFY

The Liquify filter offers a way of painting distortions into your image. As well as a creative way of distorting your image, it's also useful for adjusting shapes in images, making them thinner, fatter, or moving them to a different position.

Applying this filter makes permanent changes—in other words, you can't use it on a layer converted for Smart Filters. When you select the filter, a large dialog box appears (see below) in which you make all the adjustments. You have the option of multiple undos and to return to the original image.

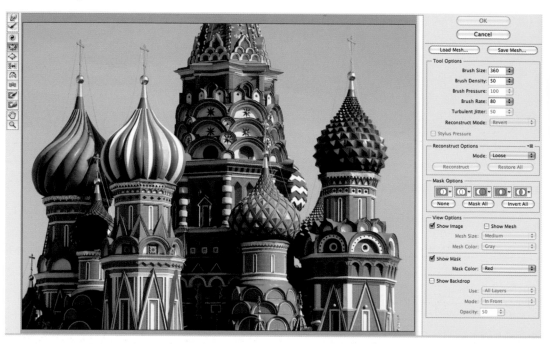

WARP TOOL

The Warp Tool is one of the most useful tools within the Liquify filter. Use it to paint in distortions, and it's easiest when beginning your distortion if you stick to a large brush.
1. Select the Warp Tool. Adjust the brush size using the [and] keys, and hold down the Shift key to increase the increments of enlarging and reducing.
2. To use the filter, click in the image and drag. It's most effective when used with short small strokes.

RECONSTRUCT TOOL

1. If you have overdone the Warp Tool, use the Reconstruct Tool to paint over the distortion and return to the original image.
2. Select the Reconstruct Tool, adjust the size of your brush (with the [and] keys), and click and drag over the elements of the image that you want to return to the original state.

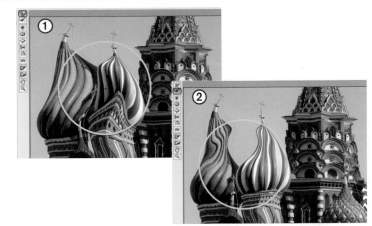

TWIRL TOOL

The Twirl Tool does as it implies—creates a twirled distortion. It works best to use it over areas that haven't already been distorted.
1. Once you've selected the Twirl Tool, adjust your Brush Size and click and hold or click and drag to create a clockwise twirl in your image. To make the twirl counterclockwise, hold down the Alt/Option key.

PUCKER TOOL

If you need to slim an area down, the Pucker Tool is very useful. It pinches an area, drawing the pixels closer together.
1. Select the Pucker Tool and click and hold—don't drag—and only hold the mouse down for a moment, otherwise you will create too much distortion.

    Hold down the Alt key to switch to the Bloat Tool (see next page).

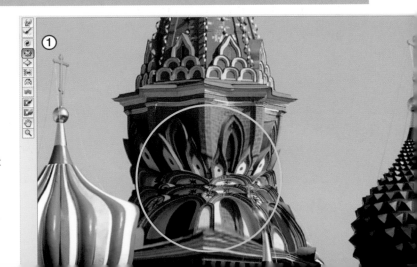

BLOAT TOOL

Producing the opposite effect to the Pucker Tool (see previous page), the Bloat Tool expands and fattens the area you "paint" over.

1. Select the Bloat Tool and click and hold. As for the Pucker Tool, drag and hold the mouse down for only a moment; otherwise, you will create too much distortion.

Hold down the Alt key to switch to the Pucker Tool (see previous page).

You can use the Bloat Tool as an easy way to enlarge an object in a photograph. In this image the dome on the right is enlarged using the Bloat Tool.

PUSH LEFT, MIRROR, AND TURBULENCE TOOLS

These tools are only useful if you want to create extreme distortions.

1. The Push Left Tool slims and narrows the detail as you drag down, and stretches and widens the pixels as you drag up. It's best used with a lower Brush Pressure (try a value of 10) for a slower, gentler slimming effect.

2. The Mirror Tool is designed to reflect the pixels you drag over.

3. Perhaps the most useful tool of these three, the Turbulence Tool creates a kind of melted effect, although it's difficult to control.

Remember you can always use the Reconstruct Tool if you get a bit carried away.

Using the Push Left Tool can be used to "slim" an object in the image.

The Mirror Tool is much harder to control, as you can see here. Unfortunately, it doesn't create a straightforward reflection.

Here the Turbulence Tool is "melting" the turrets.

ADJUSTING TOOL OPTIONS

1. You can adjust the Brush Size here or by pressing [or] on the keyboard.
2. You can adjust the Brush Density using values from 0 to 100. A lower setting creates a more concentrated effect in the center of the brush.
3. The Brush Pressure can be usefully reduced for tools that are quite strong in their application. The values range from 1 to 100.
4. The Brush Rate changes how quickly the effect is applied as you "paint."
5. You can paint more smoothly if you reduce the Turbulent Jitter.

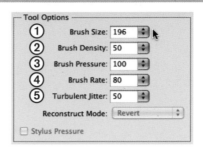

REVERTING TO THE ORIGINAL IMAGE

There are several ways to revert to the original image, although for all of them your changes will be undone and lost.
1. Hold down the Alt/Option key and press the Reset button (which has changed from Cancel). This reverts to the original image and resets all the values to default.
2. Repeatedly clicking the Reconstruct button gradually returns to the original image.
3. You can also click Restore All, which removes all the distortions but leaves any settings in place.

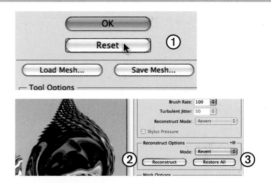

SAVING AND LOADING MESHES

You may want to save the changes you have made so far to an image and return to it later. You can do this by saving the mesh, which holds the distortions you've made.
1. You can see the mesh by checking the Show Mesh box.
2. Save the mesh by clicking Save Mesh. It will save as a .msh file.
3. Reload by clicking Load Mesh and opening the .msh file you saved before.

VANISHING POINT

Photoshop's Vanishing Point filter is a hugely powerful tool that brings 3D perspective into play. By defining planes in an image, you can then drag, merge, and paint into areas, with content kept in the same perspective plane. Copy rectangular sections in perspective and touch up with the Clone Stamp Tool, all in the Vanishing Point area.

ORIGINAL IMAGE

DEFINE A PLANE

Create Plane Tool

1. The first step requires defining a plane. With the Create Plane Tool, click four corners in a flat plane or object. The size isn't critical, just aim to get the angles right.

2. The editing process only happens within the defined plane area, so once this is created, drag the boundaries out as far as necessary using the corner and middle handles.

If the plane isn't quite accurate—that is, if the lines don't match up with the image—click and drag the corners to reshape it. Spend time getting this right, as it will control how everything else works from here.

EDITING A PLANE

Marquee
Tool

1. Select an area to change, then Ctrl/Command–drag the selection onto another area. That will be replicated within the selection. You can also use Alt/Option to drag a selection from elsewhere into a space to copy it there.

2. Use the Stamp Tool (see below) to clone areas from one place to another, keeping the perspective and distance scale correct within the defined plane. Use the Heal options (Off, Luminance, On) and the Diameter and Hardness radius settings to blend things together.

Stamp Tool

3. Zoom in to fix details with the Stamp Tool and small dragged selections, using the Feather and Opacity controls as well as the Heal settings.

MULTIPLE PLANES

1. Define two or more planes in one image either by creating each plane from scratch or by Ctrl/Command–clicking the center point in an existing plane boundary and dragging out a new one.

Step between each one by clicking into it with any editing tool. If one plane gets in the way of another, use the Edit Plane Tool to shrink it. Grab the middle of a plane border rather than a corner, and drag.

2. Select the areas you want to apply the filter to using the Selection Tool. Then, as before, hold down the Alt/Option key and drag the selection into the defined area to replicate it. Here, the building has been made taller.

3 and 4. The Vanishing Point filter puts the editing work into the current layer, so before going into the filter, make a new layer. The edits will be rendered there, making it simple to edit and mask the results back into the original image.

The building in image 3 has been extended upward—the blue sky to the left of it looks out of place with the clouds further left. In image 4 a layer mask hides the blue sky, allowing the clouds below to show through so the image is more realistic.

ADDING GRAPHICS

To add graphics from other images, copy them before selecting the Vanishing Point filter.

1. Paste, then drag the floating graphic over any perspective plane. The graphic will be put into the plane with matching perspective, and can be dragged around.

Use the Transform Tool to scale and stretch the graphic to make it fit the space, either before or after it's moved into a perspective plane.

Once placed into a perspective plane, the graphic can be moved around the entire image, even outside the defined plane area, and it will remain in relative perspective as it goes.

2. Use the Heal options to control how the new graphic blends into the image before clicking away.

If you want to render type into perspective, this must be rendered to pixels first.

Opacity: 100   Heal: On   Brush Color:

BLUR

All the Blur filters soften and defocus images, but they do so in different ways, with different kinds of controls and options—some suited to graphic manipulation, others to photographic realism.

ORIGINAL IMAGE

AVERAGE

The Average filter simply blurs the image into a single, flat, averaged-out tone and hue. There are no controls for this, so it's best used on selections when you want to convert something to a flat color based on existing content.

AVERAGE

BLUR

The basic Blur filter simply applies a slightly blurred effect to the image, with no options for controlling the extent. This reduces overall sharpness.

ORIGINAL IMAGE

BLUR

BLUR MORE

As the name implies, the Blur More filter is like the Blur filter, except that it blurs the image a little more.

BLUR MORE

BOX BLUR

Box Blur applies a basic linear blur in both horizontal and vertical directions, producing the box-like softening effect that gives this filter its name. Choosing this filter opens the Box Blur dialog box, where different blur amounts can be selected.

At low blur levels there is a look of vibration blur, as if the image were being shaken.

ORIGINAL IMAGE

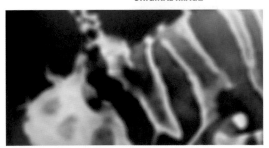

BOX BLUR SETTINGS
Radius: 3 pixels

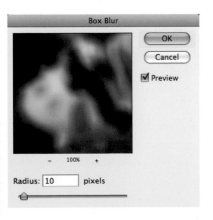

At larger blur levels there is a hazy doubling effect that can feel like the result of extreme shortsightedness.

BOX BLUR SETTINGS
Radius: 14 pixels

GAUSSIAN BLUR

Gaussian Blur is a highly controllable blurring filter that creates soft, graduated results. Use in conjunction with selections to soften areas, and with layer transparency to blend things together. Unlike the Blur and Blur More filters, which simply blur the defined edges within an image, Gaussian Blur extends the blur area so that there are no obvious start and end points to the blur.

ORIGINAL IMAGE

GAUSSIAN BLUR SETTINGS
Radius: 8 pixels

Use larger blur values to soften an image more dramatically.

GAUSSIAN BLUR SETTINGS
Radius: 15 pixels

Small values smooth out tiny details without taking away the main structure of the image.

GAUSSIAN BLUR SETTINGS
Radius: 2 pixels

LENS BLUR

The Lens Blur filter simulates the focus effects of camera lenses, a process that differs from Gaussian and other blur methods. Lens Blur uses a geometric blur that mimics the shapes of lens irises. Highlights are preserved and can be boosted if required, and transparency support allows for focus effects.

ORIGINAL IMAGE

Adding transparency or a layer mask to an image allows the Lens Blur filter to use that to mask areas in the photo. This can produce convincing shallow depth of field effects.

DEFAULT LENS BLUR SETTINGS
Shape: Hexagon (6)
Radius 15
Blade Curvature 0
Rotation 0
Brightness 0
Threshold 255
Amount 0

LENS BLUR SETTINGS
Source: Layer Mask
Blur Focal
 Distance 180
Shape: Hexagon (6)
Radius 20
Blade Curvature 0
Rotation 0
Brightness 0
Threshold 255
Amount 0

ORIGINAL IMAGE

The specular highlights in an image should normally be preserved, and the Lens Blur filter helps achieve this. By boosting Brightness and reducing Threshold levels, light areas in an image can be pushed into specular brightness.

LENS BLUR SETTINGS
Shape: Octagon (8)
Radius 10
Blade Curvature 0
Rotation 0
Brightness 5
Threshold 210
Noise 0

MOTION BLUR

This filter blurs the image in a single axis, producing a motion effect. It doesn't always produce a convincing sense of motion, partly because it blurs both ways along the axis, but it can still be very useful.

ORIGINAL IMAGE

DEFAULT MOTION BLUR SETTINGS
Angle: 0°
Distance: 10 pixels

Using a larger Distance, and setting the angle of blur to coincide with an element in the image, can produce very dramatic results.

MOTION BLUR SETTINGS
Angle: 40°
Distance: 50 pixels

Very high levels of blur make the original image impossible to make out, but the sense of directional movement is still strong.

ORIGINAL IMAGE

MOTION BLUR SETTINGS
Angle: -15°
Distance: 140 pixels

RADIAL BLUR

This filter produces a spin-effect blur, spinning or zooming around a center point. You can leave this at the center or drag the preview graphic in the filter dialog box. This doesn't give a preview of the effect, but the simple graphic representation gives a rough idea of what will happen.

ORIGINAL IMAGE

DEFAULT RADIAL BLUR SETTINGS
Amount 10
Blur Method: Spin
Quality: Good

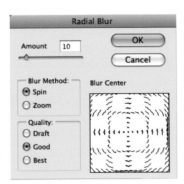

Switching to the Zoom method of blurring creates an effect like moving a zoom lens while taking a photo. A larger Amount is normally needed for this.

RADIAL BLUR SETTINGS
Amount 50
Blur Method: Zoom
Quality: Good

The Draft Quality option produces a strongly pixelated grain, the Good option gives an acceptable blur with a little grain, and the Best option takes longer but gives the smoothest results.

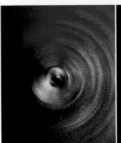 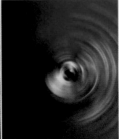 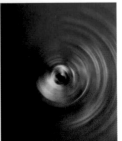

RADIAL BLUR SETTINGS
Amount 50
Blur Method: Spin
Quality: Draft

RADIAL BLUR SETTINGS
Amount 50
Blur Method: Spin
Quality: Good

RADIAL BLUR SETTINGS
Amount 50
Blur Method: Spin
Quality: Best

SHAPE BLUR

Shape Blur uses a simple graphic as the base method for the blur process. The small menu button to the right of the images allows many more to be loaded. The shape itself isn't obvious in the end result, but it does affect the output all the same.

ORIGINAL IMAGE

DEFAULT SHAPE BLUR SETTINGS
Radius: 10 pixels
Shape: Arrow 5

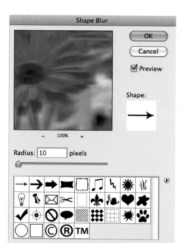

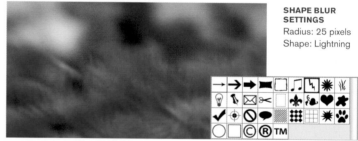

SHAPE BLUR SETTINGS
Radius: 25 pixels
Shape: Lightning

SMART BLUR

The Smart Blur filter is popular for smoothing out pores and small blemishes in skin without affecting larger details. It looks for high-contrast edges and blurs everywhere else.

ORIGINAL IMAGE

SMART BLUR SETTINGS
Radius 2.0
Threshold 25.0
Quality: Low
Mode: Normal

Increasing the Radius and Threshold levels produces a more plastic-like, illustrative result.

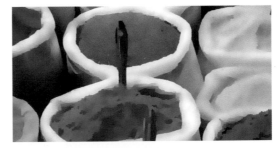

SMART BLUR SETTINGS
Radius 10.0
Threshold 50.0
Quality: High
Mode: Normal

SMART BLUR SETTINGS
Radius 10.0
Threshold 50.0
Quality: High
Mode: Overlay Edge

Changing the Mode to Edge Only or Overlay Edge draws white lines along the points of contrast where the blur effect stops. Overlay Edge also blurs the image, while Edge Only replaces it with black.

SURFACE BLUR

Surface Blur, like Smart Blur, is good for smoothing surfaces that have unwanted blemishes, whatever the image. Large and strong details are preserved while subtle marks are removed.

ORIGINAL IMAGE

DEFAULT SURFACE BLUR SETTINGS
Radius: 5 pixels
Threshold: 15 levels

DISPLACE

The Displace filter warps an image using a displacement map, to determine how the main picture is to be distorted. The map should be 50% gray where no shift is wanted, lighter or pure white for displacement in one direction, and dark or black for shifting the other way. The map can be scaled to fit the image or tiled to fill.

ORIGINAL IMAGE

MAP MAKING

To create the effect of an image printed or projected onto a rippled surface, first make a grayscale light and shade graphic. Mid-gray tones produce no movement, so start with that and paint white and black onto it, as shown here. The graphic must be saved as a Photoshop document (.psd) in order for it to work as a displacement map.

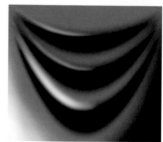

DISPLACEMENT MAP

DISPLACE WITH MAP

Select your image and go to the Displace filter. The Displace dialog box appears. When you click OK, navigate to the displacement map image. The default settings produce an equal shift horizontally and vertically, and the displacement graphic is stretched to fit the width and height of the source image.

Edges that are warped away from the border can be set to wrap around from the opposite side or repeat the edge pixels. However, layers with clear space around the image will leave undefined areas empty.

DEFAULT DISPLACE SETTINGS
Horizontal Scale 10
Vertical Scale 10
Displacement Map: Stretch To Fit
Undefined Areas: Repeat Edge Pixels

DISPLACE SETTINGS
Horizontal Scale 0
Vertical Scale 25
Displacement Map: Stretch To Fit
Undefined Areas: Repeat Edge Pixels

For a hanging drop-style effect, put more movement into the vertical scale and less into the horizontal one.

REFINING THE APPEARANCE

Once you apply the displacement, it can help tremendously to add light and shade in the appropriate areas. To do this, copy and paste the displacement map graphic onto the image (on a separate layer) and scale it to fit.

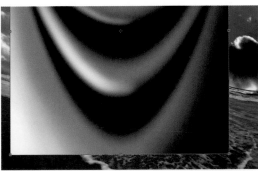

The displacement map copied and pasted onto the image.

Finally, use layer blending modes and Opacity settings to show the two layers together effectively. The Overlay blending mode works well, although it also tends to boost the saturation of images. Alternatively, try Soft Light, or Hard Light at 50% Opacity.

Using the Overlay blending mode with the displacement map on a separate layer.

PINCH

The Pinch Filter applies a distortion mesh to the image, which, by default, pinches the pixels in the center of the picture. You can't change the mesh except by using the slider, which increases the pinch if you use a positive value, or creates an inverted punched out effect if you use a negative value. It's a useful filter if you want to distort the center of an image, perhaps making it slightly larger or smaller by using low minus or plus values.

ORIGINAL IMAGE

DEFAULT PINCH
Using the default settings produces a subtle effect.

Settings
Amount 50%

PUNCH
Dragging the slider to the left, the extreme minus value creates a punched out effect. Notice the tendency for the pixels in the center to blur.

Settings
Amount -100%

DEFAULT

FILTER SETTING PARAMETERS

Amount   Min **-100%**   Max **100%**

ORIGINAL IMAGE

Settings
Amount 75%

USING THE DISTORTION

For an image that has a clear center, you can use the Pinch filter to enlarge the central area. So, for the rose on the left, using a minus value results in an enlarged center. The image above, on the other hand, has a positive value applied and the shape is less uniformly distorted.

Settings
Amount -50%

USING PUNCH

The image left is considerably distorted, although it could be used to achieve a particular effect. The picture below distorts less but still creates more emphasis on the dog's nose.

ORIGINAL IMAGE

Settings
Amount -80%

Settings
Amount -30%

POLAR COORDINATES

The Polar Coordinates filter performs a geometric distortion on an image, converting it from a rectangular to a "polar" projection—collapsing the top to a single point and wrapping the other sides around it—or unwrapping back to a rectangular projection. Use this to create planet-like images from scenic photos or cylinder anamorphic projections for viewing in curved mirrors.

ORIGINAL IMAGE

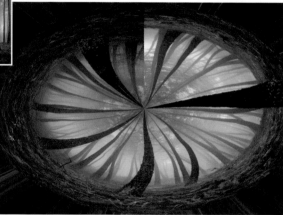

DEFAULT POLAR COORDINATES
The default behavior twists the bottom and sides of an image around the top. The corners are filled with an extrusion of the edge pixels.

Settings
Rectangular to Polar

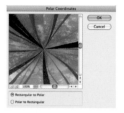

ROLL OUT
Applying the other setting, Polar to Rectangular, to an image warps the top and sides out and down and condenses the bottom inward.

Settings
Polar to Rectangular

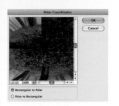

ORIGINAL IMAGE (ROTATED)

FROM ANOTHER PLANET
Left: Rotate a normal scene 180° before applying the Polar Coordinates filter, and you'll get a planet-like effect, needing just a little fixing on the seam.
Below: With a rotated image, the Polar to Rectangular variation bends the original top down into the middle.

Settings
Rectangular to Polar

Settings
Polar to Rectangular

ORIGINAL IMAGE

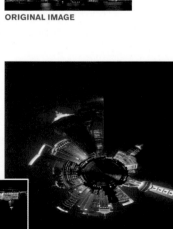

SKY SURROUND
Far left: Images with distinct sky and ground sections work well. An unrotated image will produce a tunnel-like result.
Left: Rotating the image before applying the filter creates something that appears to be floating in space. Anything that projects into the upper part of the original will be stretched out dramatically.

Settings
Rectangular to Polar

Settings
Rectangular to Polar

ORIGINAL IMAGE (ROTATED)

RIPPLE

The Ripple filter creates an undulating ripple pattern in an image, simulating ripples in liquid. There are just two controls: Size (Small, Medium, or Large), and Amount, for controlling how disturbed the surface will be. This filter is very easy to use, but if you prefer more control see the Wave filter instead (pages 364–365).

ORIGINAL IMAGE

DEFAULT RIPPLE
The default Medium Size, 100% Amount ripple produces almost no ripple at all; an almost perfectly calm day.

Settings
Amount 100%
Size Medium

GENTLE BREEZE
Switching to the Large Size but leaving the ripple Amount the same produces a slight surface disturbance. See page 17 for using masks with filters, so that you can apply this effect to the water only.

Settings
Amount 100%
Size Large

FILTER SETTING PARAMETERS

Amount   Min **-100%**   Max **100%**

ORIGINAL IMAGE

MARBLED PAINT

Left: Changing the Amount to 500% pushes the ripple effect into marbling territory, especially at the Large Size.
Below: The same 500% Amount with Small Size brings the ripple look back, to an extent at least.

Settings
Amount 500%
Size Large

Settings
Amount 500%
Size Small

ORIGINAL IMAGE

FULL EXTREMES

Far left: The ripple Amount is at the maximum 999%, so the Medium Size produces a strong effect.
Left: Adding the Large Size to the maximum ripple Amount shows the marbled effect and reveals the bidirectional mechanics of the ripple creation process.

Settings
Amount 999%
Size Medium

Settings
Amount 999%
Size Large

SHEAR

The Shear filter is a fairly simple tool; it slants your image left and right, filling in the undefined areas that open up by wrapping the image around or stretching the edge pixels across to fill. The filter is controlled by a representative adjustment line, and a preview shows the result. You can click to add more points on the Shear line.

ORIGINAL IMAGE

DEFAULT SHEAR
The standard setting for the Shear filter does nothing at all, so drag the top and bottom points of the vertical line shown in the graphic. This slants the image sideways, useful for correcting distortions or giving a sense of movement.

Settings
Drag the top right
Drag the bottom left
Undefined Areas: Wrap Around

WRAP MORE
Using a larger shear amount (dragging the line further at either end) slants the image more dramatically.

Settings
Drag the top right
Drag the bottom left
Undefined Areas: Repeat Edge Pixels

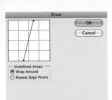

STRETCH VS. REPEAT

Left: Shear can correct some kinds of apparent distortion, for example these cyclists leaning around a corner. Note that there is no vertical correction.
Below: Uncovered areas can be filled either by wrapping the image around or by stretching the edge pixels to fill.

Settings
Undefined Areas:
Repeat Edge Pixels

ORIGINAL IMAGE

Settings
Undefined Areas: Wrap Around

CUSTOM SHEAR

Far left: Click and drag in the middle of the Shear line to create a curved Shear line, good for adding to the sensation of speed.
Left: Try adding more than one custom point to the line and drag each in different directions. The output will follow your Shear line faithfully, even when set to these extremes.

Settings
Undefined Areas:
Wrap Around

ORIGINAL IMAGE

Settings
Undefined Areas:
Wrap Around

SPHERIZE

Look into a domed mirror or the back of a spoon and you'll see the effect that the Spherize filter produces. It distorts an image as if shown on a curved surface, either as a regular spherical section or just horizontally or vertically. Adjust the distortion amount to suit your image, but remember that the more extreme values produce noticeable stretching or sphere shape clipping.

ORIGINAL IMAGE

DEFAULT SPHERIZE
At the strongest settings, this filter produces fish-eye or water-droplet distortions.

Settings
Amount 100%
Mode Normal

INVERTED EFFECT
Moving the Amount slider to a negative value shrinks the central part of the image instead.

Settings
Amount -100%
Mode Normal

FILTER SETTING PARAMETERS

Amount   Min **-100%**   Max **100%**

TALL VS. WIDE
Left: With distortion applied vertically
only, positive amounts stretch the height
of the image's center.
Below: Negative distortion amounts
squash the center of the image instead,
and produce a clearly stretched look at
the top and bottom extremes.

Settings
Amount 100%
Mode Vertical Only

ORIGINAL IMAGE

Settings
Amount -100%
Mode Vertical Only

ORIGINAL IMAGE

WIDTH-FITTING
Far left: Horizontal-only
distortion can fit an image
into a different area, and
with some subjects it can
remain looking natural.
Left: However, some kinds
of distortions make certain
kinds of objects look more
clearly incorrect.

Settings
Amount 100%
Mode Horizontal Only

Settings
Amount -100%
Mode Horizontal Only

TWIRL

The Twirl filter rotates the image, affecting the center more than the edges as it goes. There is only one control available, but the range of twirl that's available within that control is enormous: a full **999°**, or a little under three complete rotations. It's also effective at small values, giving an image a subtle twist rather than a complete spin.

ORIGINAL IMAGE

DEFAULT TWIRL
Twirl's default setting creates a slightly surrealist wobble in an image, creating a Gaudi architecture-style appearance in this image, but the filter leaves things still recognizable.

Settings
Angle 50°

TWISTER
Using a stronger Angle value for the twirl creates a more twisted result; it is less apparent what the image is, although it hasn't gone anywhere near the most extreme settings.

Settings
Angle 200°

FILTER SETTING PARAMETERS

Angle   Min **-999°**   Max **999°**

GENTLE PUSHING
Left: Tiny twirl values give an image a slight twist that is often hardly noticeable.
Below: Playing with the Angle value can generate quite comic distortions— just make sure they're appropriate for your image.

Settings
Angle 20°

ORIGINAL IMAGE

Settings
Angle 130°

ORIGINAL IMAGE

THE VORTEX
Far left: A full vortex-style twirl can be created by pulling the Angle slider all the way to the end, for the full 999° of rotation.
Left: Don't forget to try a left-handed twirl too; drag the slider left for negative twirling.

Settings
Angle -500°

Settings
Angle 999°

WAVE

Think of the Wave filter as a highly customizable and controllable form of the Ripple filter (see pages 356–357). The controls are a little complex, but the process controls a wave generator, the distance between wave peaks, the height of the waves, and the wave shape. Change one control at a time while you get used to how this works.

ORIGINAL IMAGE

DEFAULT WAVE
The default Wave settings produce quite a violent, but clearly discernible wave effect on the image, although the waves are fairly uniform in both size and shape.

Settings
Number of Generators: 5
Wavelength: Min. 10 Max. 120
Amplitude: Min. 5 Max. 35
Scale: Horiz. 100% Vert. 100%
Type: Sine
Undefined Areas:
Repeat Edge Pixels

BIG WAVES
Although the number of generators has been increased here, increasing the minimum and maximum settings for the wavelength generates fewer but more extreme waves.

Settings
Number of Generators: 17
Wavelength: Min. 267
Max. 437
Amplitude: Min. 5 Max. 35
Scale: Horiz. 100%
Vert. 100%
Type: Sine
Undefined Areas:
Repeat Edge Pixels

ONE-WAY WAVES
Left: Changing the Horizontal wave scale to 1% leaves the image fluctuating only vertically.
Below: Reducing the Vertical wave scale instead makes the image flex horizontally only, a little like a custom Shear filter setting (see pages 358–359).

Settings
Number of Generators: 17
Wavelength: Min. 267 Max. 437
Amplitude: Min. 5 Max. 35
Scale: Horiz. 1% Vert. 100%
Type: Sine
Undefined Areas: Repeat Edge Pixels

Settings
Number of Generators: 17
Wavelength: Min. 267
Max. 437
Amplitude: Min. 5 Max. 35
Scale: Horiz. 100%
Vert. 1%
Type: Sine
Undefined Areas:
Repeat Edge Pixels

ORIGINAL IMAGE

ORIGINAL IMAGE

WAVE TYPES
Far left: Changing the wave type from Sine to Triangle creates a more distorted effect.
Left: The Square wave type generates a dramatically different result; the image is broken into rectangular tiles, each of which is offset using the various other controls.

Settings
Number of Generators: 17
Wavelength: Min. 200 Max. 350
Amplitude: Min. 5 Max. 37
Scale: Horiz. 100% Vert. 100%
Type: Triangle
Undefined Areas:
Repeat Edge Pixels

Settings
Number of Generators: 5
Wavelength: Min. 200
Max. 350
Amplitude: Min. 5 Max. 37
Scale: Horiz. 100%
Vert. 100%
Type: Square
Undefined Areas:
Repeat Edge Pixels

ZIGZAG

ZigZag applies a back-and-forth distortion to the image, with a couple of options for altering the strength and one for changing the zigzag style.

ORIGINAL IMAGE

DEFAULT ZIGZAG
The default ZigZag filter settings apply a rippling effect that appears to emanate from the center of the image. The distortion is quite subtle at these settings, and the image is still fully identifiable.

Settings
Amount 10
Ridges 5
Style Pond Ripples

AROUND CENTER
Increasing the Amount (albeit to a negative value) and increasing the ridge size produces a rippled result. The image loses clarity and becomes more of a stylized graphic instead. Notice that a negative Amount rotates the opposite direction.

Settings
Amount -30
Ridges 8
Style Pond Ripples

FILTER SETTING PARAMETERS

Amount	Min **-100**	Max **100**
Ridges	Min **0**	Max **20**

GENTLE RIPPLES VS. STRONG RIPPLES

Left: The Out From Center style is rippled, but it needs heavier settings. This image has near maximum Amount.

Below: Increasing the Ridges value makes the effect much more pronounced.

Settings
Amount 90
Ridges 5
Style Out From Center

ORIGINAL IMAGE

Settings
Amount 90
Ridges 13
Style Out From Center

ORIGINAL IMAGE

Settings
Amount 15
Ridges 5
Style Around Center

REAL RIPPLES

Far left: The Around Center option applies a slightly different kind of zigzag effect. Even low values produce a dramatic result.

Left: Higher values for both Amount and Ridges deliver a dynamic whirlpool effect, reminiscent of water swirling round and down the drain.

Settings
Amount 30
Ridges 10
Style Around Center

NOISE

Noise is the name given to unwanted artifacts—usually in the form of randomly colored speckles—that occur in digital images taken in low-light conditions and with a high ISO setting. It's most noticeable in dark flat regions of an image, such as shadows. The items in the Noise section of the Filter menu help to correct damage to old photos, noise from digital cameras used in low light, and even the patterning and moiré caused by scanning halftone-printed images from magazines.

ORIGINAL IMAGE

ADD NOISE

Adding noise to an image may seem odd, but this is a good way to make a gradient or over-smoothed image look a little more natural, or at least less flat.

DEFAULT ADD NOISE SETTINGS
Amount: 12.5%
Distribution Uniform

If the default RGB noise is too colorful, the Monochromatic option will apply a tonal-only noise pattern instead. Use the Gaussian distribution to add more of the noise in the midtones than in the light or dark extremes.

ADD NOISE SETTINGS
Amount: 12.5%
Distribution Gaussian
Monochromatic

DESPECKLE

Despeckle is a one-shot filter, useful for removing visual patterns such as halftone dot screens from images scanned from print. There are no options for controlling this, so if it doesn't produce the right result, move on to a different filter.

ORIGINAL IMAGE
(enlarged detail)

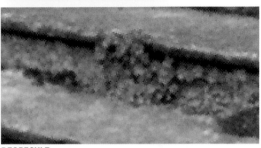

DESPECKLE

DUST & SCRATCHES

Images with dust marks and scratches, for example old prints or negatives that you've scanned, can be healed surprisingly effectively with the Dust & Scratches filter, but beware of losing important details.

ORIGINAL IMAGE

DEFAULT DUST & SCRATCHES SETTINGS
Radius: 1 pixel
Threshold: 0 levels

DUST & SCRATCHES SETTINGS
Radius: 5 pixels
Threshold: 50 levels

Increasing the Radius will deal with larger flaws, but it will also affect image detail. Try raising the Threshold level to prevent too much detail from being treated as dust or scratch marks and blurred out altogether.

MEDIAN

The Median filter is a useful tool for removing noise and grain texture from skin and similar surfaces. It has just one control, the Radius slider, and it blurs detail while trying to preserve overall shapes.

ORIGINAL IMAGE

DEFAULT MEDIAN SETTINGS
Radius: 1 pixel

At larger than default Radius settings, the Median filter softens all details, but the basic shape-preserving abilities help to maintain the general look of the image.

MEDIAN SETTINGS
Radius: 5 pixels

REDUCE NOISE

The Reduce Noise filter is a flexible way to reduce image noise, whether it's from film grain, digital noise, or scanner artifacts. In this series of images, the standard settings have made little impact on the noise. Overdo the settings, however, and the image appears plastic (middle). The bottom image is a compromise and provides the best result.

ORIGINAL IMAGE

If the image shows JPEG color artifacts, enable the Remove JPEG Artifact option; this helps minimize the color blocks introduced by heavy JPEG compression. The Reduce Color Noise slider is better for dealing with digital photo noise.

DEFAULT REDUCE NOISE SETTINGS
Strength: 6
Preserve Details: 60%
Reduce Color Noise: 45%
Sharpen Details: 25%

REDUCE NOISE SETTINGS
Strength: 10
Preserve Details: 0%
Reduce Color Noise: 100%
Sharpen Details: 0%
Remove JPEG Artifact

Choose the Advanced option and you can add setting per color channel of the image as well as overall. These are applied on top of the options chosen in the Overall section.

REDUCE NOISE SETTINGS
Strength: 9
Preserve Details: 30%
Reduce Color Noise: 70%
Sharpen Details: 50%
Remove JPEG Artifact
Advanced (Green Channel)
Strength: 7
Preserve Details: 11%

CRYSTALLIZE

The Crystallize filter reproduces images as if painted with solid dabs of paint, or flat, colored facets. At low Cell Size levels, the effect is a subtle mottling, whereas at larger sizes it becomes more abstract and unfocused. Whatever settings you choose, use this filter to create an Impressionist effect.

ORIGINAL IMAGE

DEFAULT CRYSTALLIZE
The default setting produces dabs of color that break up fine detail in the image yet preserve the structure fairly well. This is a quick and easy way to fake an Impressionist-style image.

Settings
Cell Size 10

BIGGER BLOCKS
Pushing the Cell Size value up a little from the default creates a more abstract result, replacing tonal detail with abstract color daubs.

Settings
Cell Size 25

ORIGINAL IMAGE

LEVELS OF ABSTRACTION

Left: Large cell sizes increase the abstract effect, taking it to the edge of recognizability.

Below: Very large cell sizes deliver randomly shaped blocks of color derived loosely from the hues of the original image.

Settings
Cell Size 50

Settings
Cell Size 100

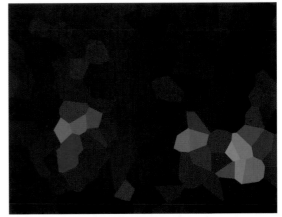

ORIGINAL IMAGE

Settings
Cell Size 7

PRESERVING DETAIL

Far left: Using smaller rather than larger cell sizes preserves the image detail while still generating a subtle paint-like effect.

Left: At the smallest possible Cell Size, the image is hardly different from the original, but there is still a slight, and potentially useful, impact.

Settings
Cell Size 3

FACET

The Facet filter is one of the one-shot variety; it has no settings to control the degree of the filter effect. This simply creates small blocks in the image based on the original color and brightness values and the contrast shapes. Fine detail is replaced by a subtle, mottled effect. How strong the effect depends on the image's resolution.

ORIGINAL IMAGE

FACET
Left and below: Areas of fine detail in these images have been replaced by faceted cells based on the same brightness and hue, but the images remain largely the same.

ORIGINAL IMAGE

FRAGMENT

Like the Facet filter, Fragment has no settings to alter. This filter simply creates four copies of the original image, offset relative to each other and made slightly translucent. The result is a fragmented blur—the lower the image resolution, the greater the blur effect.

ORIGINAL IMAGE

FRAGMENT
Left and below: By creating a four-way offset of the original image, the Fragment filter creates an effect a little like an omnidirectional vibration blur, as if from a camera placed on a running motor.

ORIGINAL IMAGE

MEZZOTINT

A mezzotint is a method of reproducing an image in print using etched strokes or spots, rather than the more common halftone dots. Photoshop's Mezzotint filter takes this idea and turns it into an effects filter, reproducing an image in a high-contrast, colorful simulation of this process.

ORIGINAL IMAGE

DEFAULT MEZZOTINT
The default Mezzotint effect is Fine Dots. This simply applies a fine dot-style etch effect to the different color channels of the image.

Settings
Type Fine Dots

COARSE DOTS
At the other end of the dot-style scale, past Medium and Grainy, lies Coarse Dots, a high-contrast effect that greatly exaggerates the appearance of the individual color channels.

Settings
Type Coarse Dots

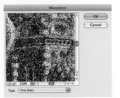

SHORT VS. LONG LINES

Left: The Short Lines form of the Mezzotint effect breaks up detail with high-contrast strokes.
Below: Using the Long Lines setting produces a more graphic, almost screenprinted effect.

ORIGINAL IMAGE

Settings
Type Short Lines

Settings
Type Long Lines

ORIGINAL IMAGE

STROKES

Far left: The Strokes setting produces a relatively traditional etched-line mezzotint appearance.
Left: Using longer strokes exaggerates the graphic effect.

Settings
Type Short Strokes

Settings
Type Long Strokes

MOSAIC

The Mosaic filter does just one job: it creates a crisp, pixelated appearance from images, making them look stylishly low resolution. This is a much cleaner effect than simply resizing and resampling an image, so for pixelated blocks, fake it this way.

ORIGINAL IMAGE

DEFAULT MOSAIC
The default Mosaic filter setting creates an obviously pixelated image but one that still retains a fair amount of detail.

Settings
Cell Size: 8 square

LOSING DETAIL
Double the Cell Size and the Mosaic filter starts to eliminate detail.

Settings
Cell Size: 16 square

FILTER SETTING PARAMETERS

Cell Size: Min **2 square**   Max **200 square**

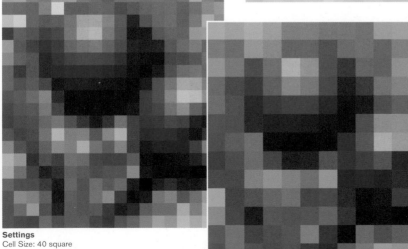

PROGRESSIVE BLOCKS

Left: At three times the default Cell Size setting, results are graphic.
Below: The detail is all but gone here; the image is recognizable, but only just.

ORIGINAL IMAGE

Settings
Cell Size: 24 square

Settings
Cell Size: 32 square

ORIGINAL IMAGE

ABSTRACT BLOCKS

Far left: This setting shows how abstract the Mosaic filter results can appear.
Left: It's easy to take an image beyond all chance of recognition, turning it into an averaged-out grid of colored squares.

Settings
Cell Size: 40 square

Settings
Cell Size: 60 square

POINTILLIZE

The Pointillize filter breaks the image up into discrete dots that are colored according to the hues and shades of the original image. The spaces between and behind the dots are filled with the current background color as set in the Tools panel.

ORIGINAL IMAGE

DEFAULT POINTILLIZE
The Pointillize filter's default settings produce small dots similar to the effect developed by Georges Seurat in the late 19th century.

Settings
Cell Size 5

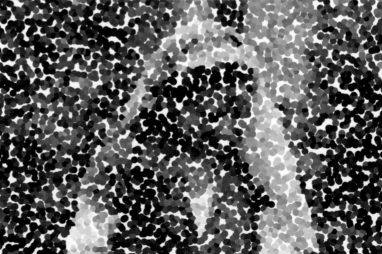

SCALING THE DOTS
Increasing the dot size a little will lose more detail, but the feel remains largely the same at this level.

Settings
Cell Size 15

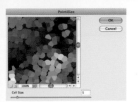

FILTER SETTING PARAMETERS

Cell Size	Min **3**	Max **300**

TURNING ABSTRACT

Left: As the Cell Size increases, the original image becomes harder to decipher.

Below: Eventually it becomes impressionistic and almost nothing else. Remember to change the background color to control what lies behind the dots.

Settings
Cell Size 25

ORIGINAL IMAGE

Settings
Cell Size 35

PURE ABSTRACTION

Far left: Increase the Cell Size further to create abstract dot patterns from an image.

Left: By making the dots far too big to deliver any image detail at all, you're left with a dramatic flat color abstraction in one easy step.

Settings
Cell Size 60

Settings
Cell Size 100

CLOUDS

The Clouds filter uses the Foreground and Background Colors to replace the image with clouds. If you hold down the Alt/Option key, you can produce clouds with more contrast. The filter is most useful to add texture to areas of sky.

ORIGINAL IMAGE

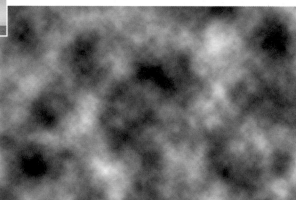

DEFAULT CLOUDS
With the default Foreground/ Background colors of black and white, respectively, the filter covers up the original image entirely with white clouds on a gray to black background.

Foreground/ Background Colors

CLOUDS
New Foreground and Background Colors were chosen from the image (see below) before the Clouds filter was applied to a new layer. The Multiply blending mode was then selected for the new layer, giving this effect.

Foreground/ Background Colors

DIFFERENCE CLOUDS

This filter leaves more of the original image intact. Very simply, it still applies the Clouds filter but then fades it by applying the Difference blending mode, producing strong color swings. The effect is changed according to the Foreground and Background Colors you choose.

ORIGINAL IMAGE

Foreground/
Background
Colors

DEFAULT DIFFERENCE CLOUDS
You can still see some of the cloud pattern as the clouds—here with default Foreground/Background colors—and the original image blend together.

ORIGINAL IMAGE

Foreground/
Background
Colors

DIFFERENCE CLOUDS
The Foreground/Background Colors are rendered as they would appear under the Difference blending mode.

FIBERS AND LENS FLARE

Both the Fiber and Lens Flare filters, in the Render filters category, generate graphic effects that can be worked into other images. Both filters must be applied to layers with image content, as they can't work on empty layers. However, Fibers takes over the image, so you'll need to use layer blending methods to work it into an existing image.

ORIGINAL IMAGE

FIBERS

With default Foreground and Background Colors (black and white), the Fibers filter generates a monochrome stranded fiber effect, stretched vertically down your image. The same pattern is generated no matter what the content of your original image. Click the Randomize button to generate new fibers using the current settings.

Foreground/
Background
Colors

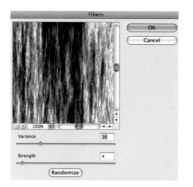

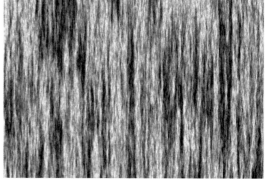

DEFAULT FIBERS SETTINGS
Variance 16
Strength 4

The Variance slider increases the contrast of the fibers, and the Strength slider increases the frequency from fairly lumpy to fine, frequent strips. Here, alternative Foreground and Background Colors have been applied.

Alternative Foreground/
Background Colors

FIBERS SETTINGS
Variance 4
Strength 3

LENS FLARE

You can simulate the effect of light flare in camera lenses with the Lens Flare filter. A bright light point and corresponding lens flare halo is generated in the current image layer. Drag the light point around in the small preview to position this as needed in your image.

LENS FLARE SETTINGS
Brightness: 100%
Lens Type
50–300mm Zoom

If you push the Brightness level higher than 100%, you can blast the image with light and increase the lens flare halo effects.

LENS FLARE SETTINGS
Brightness: 130%
Lens Type 35mm Prime

The Movie Prime lens type produces a strip-style lens flare rather than the more common style of the other options.

LENS FLARE SETTINGS
Brightness: 130%
Lens Type Movie Prime

SHARPEN

Photoshop's various Sharpen filters are very useful. They can rescue a soft image and add sparkle to an otherwise flat photo, and they can increase the contrast and punch.

The Sharpen filters can't add detail that isn't in the original image, but they can make pictures look sharper. It's good practice to view the image at Actual Pixel size when applying any sharpening filter.

ORIGINAL IMAGE

SHARPEN

The basic Sharpen filter doesn't have any controls; it just applies a single sharpening effect. If this isn't what you want, then the other filters should help.

SHARPEN

SHARPEN EDGES

Sharpen Edges concentrates its effects where the image has defined edges, boosting their contrast while leaving other areas alone. This prevents sharpening being applied to areas of flat tone that may exhibit more noise than detailed areas.

SHARPEN EDGES

SHARPEN MORE

If you want something a little stronger than Sharpen or Sharpen Edges, the Sharpen More filter might be ideal. It applies a more defined sharpening effect than the previous two, but again offers no level of control.

SHARPEN MORE

SMART SHARPEN

The Smart Sharpen filter gives more control over both the level of sharpening and what is and isn't affected by the filter. It can be fine-tuned to remove Gaussian Blur, Lens Blur, or Motion Blur, with sliders for the sharpness Amount and Radius (how large an area is affected).

DEFAULT SMART SHARPEN SETTINGS
Amount: 100%
Radius: 1.0 px
Remove: Gaussian Blur

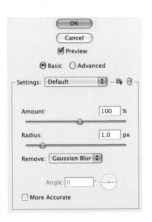

SMART SHARPEN SETTINGS
Amount: 140%
Radius: 3.0 px
Remove: Lens Blur

Larger sharpening amounts and a bigger radius gives an image even more punch, although it will start to look artificial if taken too far.

SMART SHARPEN: ADVANCED

The Advanced option in the Smart Sharpen dialog box has separate controls for shadow and highlight sharpening. These are applied on top of the standard Sharpen settings, allowing more effective sharpening without over exaggerating contrast, and for applying more sharpening in the highlights than the shadows or vice versa.

SMART SHARPEN SETTINGS

Amount: 140%
Radius: 3.0 px
Remove: Lens Blur
Shadow Fade Amount: 50%
Shadow Tonal Width: 50%

Shadow Radius: 1 px
Highlight Fade Amount: 60%
Highlight Tonal Width: 74%
Highlight Radius: 1

By boosting the controls for the highlight areas and reducing them for the shadows, the hairlike parts of this flower have been pulled out strongly without over sharpening the darker parts of the image.

ORIGINAL IMAGE

SMART SHARPEN SETTINGS

Amount: 140%
Radius: 3.0 px
Remove: Gaussian Blur
Shadow Fade Amount: 100%
Shadow Tonal Width: 80%

Shadow Radius: 1 px
Highlight Fade Amount: 40%
Highlight Tonal Width: 40%
Highlight Radius: 80

UNSHARP MASK

The Unsharp Mask filter doesn't sound like a good sharpening choice, but it's named for the way it defines the areas to be sharpened. It creates a blurred mask that protects areas that don't have particularly high contrast, and then exaggerates the light and dark values along those contrast borders. The Radius controls the breadth of the sharpened area, and the Threshold controls how much contrast difference is allowed before it's considered ready for sharpening.

DEFAULT UNSHARP MASK SETTINGS
Amount: 50%
Radius: 1.0 pixels
Threshold: 0 levels

Increase the Amount and Radius to push the sharpening level up, and boost the Threshold level to prevent minor tone steps from being sharpened as well.

UNSHARP MASK SETTINGS
Amount: 110%
Radius: 2.0 pixels
Threshold: 10 levels

Push the Radius slider up to very high levels so that the sharpening area is increased. The result pumps the image with light and life, although at the expense of a slight loss of detail.

UNSHARP MASK SETTINGS
Amount: 110%
Radius: 60 pixels
Threshold: 20 levels

DIFFUSE

The Diffuse filter mimics looking at an image through slightly frosted glass. It can be quite subtle, so you may find that applying the filter a number of times is helpful. With the settings, edges are broken up in a slightly frosted, speckled manner, while the softening Anisotropic option is a very useful tool for creating a "retouched photo model" look with skin.

ORIGINAL IMAGE

DEFAULT DIFFUSE
With the Mode set to Normal, the diffusion effect breaks up tones using both lightening and darkening methods. Use Ctrl/Cmd-F to reapply the filter.

Settings
Mode Normal

DARK DIFFUSION
Set the filter's Mode to Darken Only and highlight edges will be far less affected.

Settings
Mode Darken Only

ANISOTROPIC DIFFUSION

Left: Skin tones and some other subjects suit the Anisotropic soft diffusion well as it covers up blemishes without removing too much detail.
Below: Not all images benefit from this; notice how architectural detail here has been softened.

Settings
Mode Anisotropic

ORIGINAL IMAGE

ORIGINAL IMAGE

Settings
Mode Anisotropic

HIGH CONTRAST

Far left: The diffusion effect is most obvious on high-contrast edges.
Left: Choosing the Lighten Only Mode helps control the effect, although it can lose lighter detail.

Settings
Mode Lighten Only

Settings
Mode Normal

EMBOSS

The Emboss filter creates a raised effect by converting an image's fill to a neutral gray, putting highlights and shadows around high-contrast edges, and overlaying tinted and inverted versions of the original image colors. Used on duplicate image layers with the Overlay blending mode, this filter can provide a powerful alternative method of sharpening.

ORIGINAL IMAGE

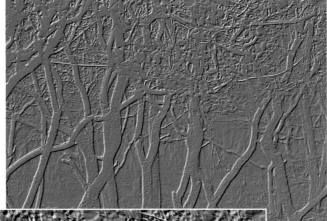

DEFAULT EMBOSS
The default Emboss settings produce a gray image with highlights, shadow lines, and hints of color derived from the original scene.

Settings
Angle: 135°
Height: 3 pixels
Amount: 100%

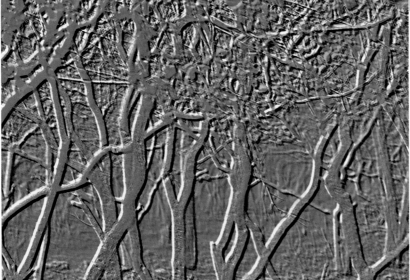

BIGGER EMBOSS
Changing nothing but the Height setting produces a more contrasting version of the original that features more pronounced colors.

Settings
Angle: 135°
Height: 8 pixels
Amount: 100%

FILTER SETTING PARAMETERS

Height: Min **1 pixel**   Max **100 pixels**

Amount: Min **1%**   Max **500%**

EXTREME OFFSETS

Left: Change Angle to 90° and increase both Height and Amount. The result looks less like embossing, but it's powerful nonetheless.
Below: Using an extreme Height (offset shift) changes the appearance dramatically, with a rainbow of color portraying a collage effect.

ORIGINAL IMAGE

Settings
Angle: 90°
Height: 10
Amount: 200%

Settings
Angle: 90°
Height: 50
Amount: 200%

ORIGINAL IMAGE

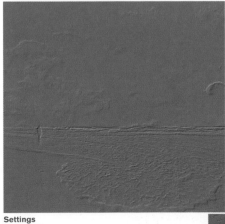

SUBTLE EMBOSSING

Far left: Using a very low Height leaves the image largely gray, picking out only the strongest edge contrasts.
Left: The maximum Emboss Amount possible has been applied here to bring out the detail. The result is rather metallic, but when blended with other layers it can transform an image in many ways.

Settings
Angle: -45°
Height: 1 pixel
Amount: 500%

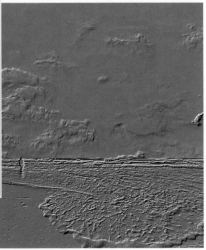

Settings
Angle: -45°
Height: 1 pixel
Amount: 100%

EXTRUDE

The Extrude filter turns an image into a simulated 3D extrusion of shapes and colors taken from the original image. You have a fair amount of control over the way this extrusion happens, although much of how the end result works is taken from the source image. This is good for dramatic effect or as one of the stages in a graphically rich set of image manipulations.

ORIGINAL IMAGE

DEFAULT EXTRUDE
The standard form of the Extrude effect produces a random-height array of blocks, like 3D pixelation. Each block is colored according to the corresponding part of the original image, but the result is highly abstract.

Settings
Type: Blocks
Size: 30 Pixels
Depth: 30 Random

PYRAMID
Switching Extrude Type to Pyramids turns the block output to four-sided pyramid shapes.

Settings
Type: Pyramids
Size: 30 Pixels
Depth: 30 Random

Extrude
Type: ● Blocks ○ Pyramids   [OK]
Size: 30 Pixels   [Cancel]
Depth: 30 ● Random ○ Level-based
☐ Solid Front Faces
☐ Mask Incomplete Blocks

FILTER SETTING PARAMETERS

Size:	Min **2 Pixels**	Max **255 Pixels**
Depth:	Min **1**	Max **255**

TINY BLOCKS

Left: Smaller blocks with the depth taken from the brightness values create a rather different feel. With the Solid Front Faces option selected, the front block face becomes flat color.
Below: Reducing Size to its minimum makes a near-perfect 3D pixel storm. Experiment with Depth amounts.

Settings
Type: Blocks
Size: 10 Pixels
Depth: 60 Level-based
Solid Front Faces

ORIGINAL IMAGE

Settings
Type: Blocks
Size: 2 Pixels
Depth: 60 Level-based
Solid Front Faces

ORIGINAL IMAGE

3D CLIPPING

Far left: The Mask Incomplete Blocks option removes any blocks that don't fit within the document area, showing the original image instead.
Left: Unchecking the Solid Front Faces option puts the original image onto the front face of every block, helping to hint at the original image in the main areas.

Settings
Type: Blocks
Size: 15 Pixels
Depth: 255 Level-based
Mask Incomplete Blocks

Settings
Type: Blocks
Size: 15 Pixels
Depth: 100 Random
Solid Front Faces
Mask Incomplete Blocks

FIND EDGES

The Find Edges filter has no adjustable controls. It finds areas in an image that have significant contrast changes and emphasizes those edges, dramatically, with color and dark lines. The rest of the image is turned white, creating a distinctive illustrative version of the original picture.

ORIGINAL IMAGE

DRAWN EDGES
Images with lots of contrasting detail will produce a large number of outline edges. The use of black and colored lines on a white ground can appear to be in negative, so try inverting the image afterward.

FIND EDGES

SOLARIZE

Solarizing is an old photographic process where overexposing a print inverts highlight areas while leaving darker areas alone. Photoshop's Solarize filter does the same, inverting both tone and color in light areas while leaving dark areas as they are in the original image.

ORIGINAL IMAGE

SIMPLE SOLARIZE
Applying the Solarize filter to an image with many white areas will create a much darker image as a result. Light and midtoned colors are inverted, but dark tones and hues in the original image remain unchanged.

SOLARIZE

TILES

The Tiles filter slices the image into regular sections and applies a random offset to each one. On top of the choice for the Number Of Tiles (which is counted vertically) and the Maximum Offset in percentage of tile size, the area behind the tiles can be filled in a number of different ways.

ORIGINAL IMAGE

Foreground/
Background
Colors

DEFAULT TILES
The default Tiles settings produce an array of ten tiles to fill the height of the image, with 10% Offset, and with the empty area behind the shifted tiles filled with the current Background Color (left) or the Foreground Color (below).

Settings
Number of Tiles: 10
Maximum Offset: 10%
Fill Empty Area With:
Background Color

Settings
Number of Tiles: 10
Maximum Offset: 10%
Fill Empty Area With:
Foreground Color

FILTER SETTING PARAMETERS

Number Of Tiles:	Min **1**		Max **99%**
Maximum Offset:	Min **1%**		Max **99%**

ORIGINAL IMAGE

Settings
Number of Tiles: 50
Maximum Offset: 50%
Fill Empty Area With: Inverse Image

SMALLER TILES
Above: With a higher
Number Of Tiles and higher
Offset setting, the image
becomes harder to read,
particularly with the
Fill Empty Area With:
Inverse Image option.
Left: Setting Number of
Tiles to 2 produces a
seemingly random choice
of image elements.

Settings
Number of Tiles: 2
Maximum Offset: 30%
Fill Empty Area With:
Background Color

Settings
Number of Tiles: 10
Maximum Offset: 50%
Fill Empty Area With:
Unaltered Image

ORIGINAL IMAGE

BACKGROUNDS
Far left: Using Unaltered
Image as the background
behind the tiles produces a
subtly fragmented output.
Left: Using the maximum
allowed Offset (99%)
shuffles the tiles around a
lot more than the default
settings, breaking up the
image.

Settings
Number of Tiles: 20
Maximum Offset: 99%
Fill Empty Area With:
Background Color

TRACE CONTOUR

Trace Contour simply draws lines along edges of a particular brightness level in an image, using colors derived from the image to generate one-pixel-width strokes. The brightness level can be set from 0 to 255, with 128 being the midpoint.

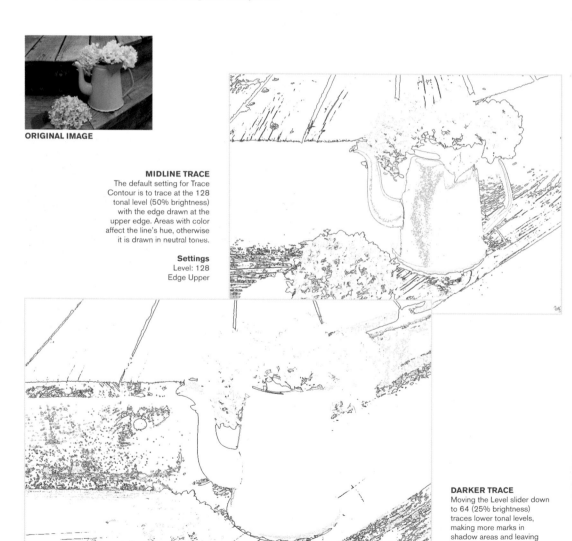

ORIGINAL IMAGE

MIDLINE TRACE
The default setting for Trace Contour is to trace at the 128 tonal level (50% brightness) with the edge drawn at the upper edge. Areas with color affect the line's hue, otherwise it is drawn in neutral tones.

Settings
Level: 128
Edge Upper

DARKER TRACE
Moving the Level slider down to 64 (25% brightness) traces lower tonal levels, making more marks in shadow areas and leaving the lighter spaces empty.

Settings
Level: 64
Edge Upper

FILTER SETTING PARAMETERS

Level: Min **0**   Max **255**

MULTIPLE LINES
Left: Applying the filter multiple times produces a halo of lines, each drawn offset from the edge of the previous.
Below: As with many filters, one effective use is to blend with an unfiltered copy of the image.

Settings
Level: 128
Edge Upper

ORIGINAL IMAGE

Settings
Level: 128
Edge Upper
(Layer Blend Mode Overlay)

Settings
Level: 147
Edge Lower

EXTRACTING DETAIL
Far left: Different tonal levels will pull out different details from an image. At 147, the skateboard is clearly defined.
Left: Sliding the level down to 70 means that the figure is effectively isolated and the skateboard has all but disappeared.

Settings
Level: 70
Edge Lower

WIND

Applying a pixel-based wind effect is the job of the Wind filter. This offers three strengths of wind, plus a choice of direction. The default settings produce a smoothly blended effect that blows highlight streaks across shadow areas, but there are stronger, more graphic options available as well.

ORIGINAL IMAGE

DEFAULT WIND
The Wind filter's default Wind setting produces a relatively fine and blended look where light edges can be blown across darker areas. Note that dark tones never get blown into lighter ones.

Settings
Method Wind
Direction From the Right

WIND BLASTED
The Blast method causes a visually harsher effect. It's essentially the same as the basic Wind method, but there is no blending of the pixel streaks into the image background.

Settings
Method Blast
Direction From the Right

PHOTOGRAPHIC VS. GRAPHIC
Left: The Wind method and an appropriate direction adds a feeling of speed in a near realistic manner.
Below: The Blast method is far more obviously graphic; highlights bleed crisply and dark details are obliterated.

ORIGINAL IMAGE

Settings
Method Wind
Direction From the Left

ORIGINAL IMAGE

Settings
Method Blast
Direction From the Left

STAGGER BLEED
Far left: The Stagger method blows dark areas into light as well as light into dark, breaking up images in a distinctive way.
Left: Stagger can break up and distort important parts of an image, so use it with caution.

Settings
Method Stagger
Direction From the Left

Settings
Method Stagger
Direction From the Right

VIDEO

The De-Interlace filter can help transform the odd/even field oddities found in images captured from interlaced video sources into more normal images. If you create graphics for use in video, the NTSC Colors filter can help control the saturation, preventing color bleeding when broadcast.

ORIGINAL IMAGE

DE-INTERLACE

Video that has unsightly offset even and odd horizontal fields needs to be de-interlaced. The filter can remove the odd or even fields and create new lines from what's left. Duplication is the default, doubling up the rows of pixels.

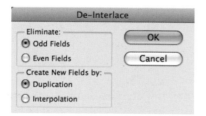

DE-INTERLACE SETTINGS
Eliminate: Odd Fields
Create New Fields by: Duplication

Creating new fields by Interpolation is generally a better option as it produces a slightly softer, blended result.

DE-INTERLACE SETTINGS
Eliminate: Odd Fields
Create New Fields by: Interpolation

NTSC COLORS

Fully saturated colors from computer graphics that overlay the TV picture are likely to bleed unpleasantly when shown on regular TV displays. This filter gently desaturates problematic color saturation extremes to avoid this issue. No controls are available; it just does its job in one hit.

OTHER

The filters in Photoshop's "Other" section are the ones that can't easily be categorized elsewhere. Some, like Offset (see pages 410–411), aren't at all hard to use, while Custom falls at the other end of the usability spectrum.

ORIGINAL IMAGE

CUSTOM

The Custom filter lets users create their own filter effects. The downside, however, is that it's done entirely through arrays of numeric values (see below), each cell being a pixel-level operation. It's powerful but obscure—but at least you can save and load your own experimental settings.

CUSTOM DIALOG BOX

CUSTOM SETTINGS
0,0,0,0,0
0,0,-1,0,0
-2,-1,10,-1,-2
0,0,-1,0,0
0,0,0,0,0

Scale: 1
Offset: 0

HIGH PASS

The High Pass filter preserves sharp color changes and knocks back anything else in an image, eliminating small details. It isn't very useful on its own, but try applying a Threshold conversion afterward.

THRESHOLD CONVERSION APPLIED

HIGH PASS SETTINGS
Radius 10

MAXIMUM AND MINIMUM

The Maximum and Minimum filters are used mainly for modifying layer masks and alpha channels. Maximum enlarges the white areas, choking into the black, while Minimum does the opposite, spreading out the black areas and reducing the area of white. It produces interesting effects when applied to full-color images, but it doesn't take much radius enlargement before it transforms images into abstract artworks.

MAXIMUM SETTINGS
Radius: 2

MINIMUM SETTINGS
Radius: 2

MAXIMUM SETTINGS
Radius: 2

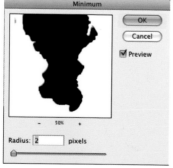

MINIMUM SETTINGS
Radius: 2

These two bottom images show the effect of the filter on a layer mask.

DIGIMARC

If you've ever worried about your images being used without permission, then you should try out the Digimarc filter. This doesn't prevent someone from copying an image, but it does ensure that there is a small amount of copyright information embedded invisibly—but retrievably—in your pictures. If someone checks for Digimarc data in Photoshop, it will be found, even if the picture has been through a certain amount of image manipulation. It doesn't guarantee that everyone will behave themselves, but it helps prove your ownership if the need arises.

Once an image is watermarked, you can check it using the Read Watermark filter in the Digimarc filter section.

The Digimarc filter bundled with Photoshop puts a copyright year and some generic notices into the watermark. If you want to add more detail to the encoded data, you'll need to sign up for Digimarc's commercial services.

The Digimarc filter works by embedding data encoded as a very subtle tone and hue pattern into the image. The strength of the visual effect is determined by the Durability value. The lower the value, the easier it is for someone to remove the visual watermark. Although the visual effect is almost undetectable, it's sensible to keep originals unwatermarked.

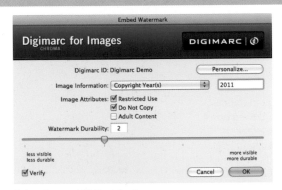

Select the type of information to embed, along with its durability.

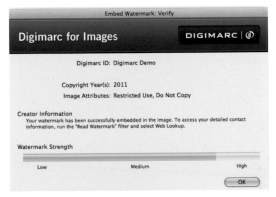

Once you've embedded the information, a window will inform you that your image is digitally watermarked.

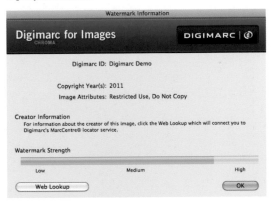

You can also find out about an image's copyright using the Read Watermark element of the Digimarc filter.

OFFSET

Photoshop's Offset filter is not a particularly complex feature, but it can be more useful than most people realize. Use it to wrap images around, putting the original edges into the center, then clone-stamp the visible edge away. The result is a seamless, tiled image. The option to repeat the edge pixels is more graphic than photographic, but also useful.

ORIGINAL IMAGE

HORIZONTAL SHIFT
Offset an image horizontally with the Wrap Around option selected, and the sides are moved to the middle. Basic image editing can hide this seam, preparing the image for tiling in Web and print designs.

Settings
Horizontal: 600 pixels right
Vertical: 0 pixels down
Undefined Areas
Wrap Around

ORIGINAL IMAGE

BOTH WAYS
This image has been offset in both directions at once to split the image into four sections. If you want two-way tiling, do the offset one direction at a time rather than like this.

Settings
Horizontal: 600 pixels right
Vertical: 400 pixels down
Undefined Areas
Wrap Around

REPEAT EDGE PIXELS

Left: Repeating the edge pixels instead of wrapping around produces a stylized graphic look.
Below: Offset in two directions with Repeat Edge Pixels, and the quadrant opposite the image will be filled with the color of the nearest corner image pixel.

Settings
Horizontal: 600 pixels right
Vertical: 0 pixels down
Undefined Areas
Repeat Edge Pixels

Settings
Horizontal: 300 pixels right
Vertical: -200 pixels down
Undefined Areas
Repeat Edge Pixels

STRAIGHT UP

Far left: Vertical-only offset can be used to create a vertically tiling image. This requires only a little manual editing to make the join seamless.
Left: By extending the edge pixels into the offset space, flat areas such as sky can be extended, but beware of subtle pixel-level differences causing streaks.

Settings
Horizontal: 0 pixels right
Vertical: 500 pixels down
Undefined Areas Wrap Around

ORIGINAL IMAGE

ORIGINAL IMAGE

Settings
Horizontal: 0 pixels right
Vertical: 500 pixels down
Undefined Areas
Repeat Edge Pixels

INDEX

CREDITS

The idea to create a directory showing the effects of each of the Photoshop filters was that of Moira Clinch, Creative Director at Quarto, so more than thanks go to her, since without her the book would not exist.

The person who has held everything together, nursing the book through its stages of production like a careful midwife, is Katie Crous, Senior Editor at Quarto. That this book exists is as much down to her work as any author's!

I would also like to thank Steve Luck, the Technical Editor, who embraced the systematic checking of all the settings and other technical details, playing a vital role in ensuring the book's usefulness, and acting as a contributor to boot.

The work of writing and producing this book is also down to the other contributors: Keith Martin in particular, who wrote much of the Other Filter Effects section; and Kevin Curtis.

Quarto would like to thank:
Steve Luck, especially for compiling and writing the following pages: 208–209, 212–213, 216–217, 220–221, 224–225, 228–229, 232–233, 236–237, 240–241, 246–247, 252–253, 256–257, 262–263, 266–267, 270–271, 274–275.

Sergey Skleznev p14, 103, 343, 347, 363
Fotolistic p18, 248, 312, 362, 374
Dania Lee p20, 99
Pirita p21, 44, 217
Toth Tamas p23, 65, 252
James Steidl p32, 126, 302, 384
RoxyFer p33, 154, 289, 307
Vinicius Tupinamba p36,
inacio pires p37, 57, 96, 143, 313, 392, 352, 385
Ammit p37, 192, 267
Maridav p40, 308
Hashim Pudiyapura p42, 151, 349, 365
Tramper p45, 213, 372
WDG Photo p46
Salajean p48, 170, 325
Severe p49
Angel_A p49, 165
Digitalsport-photoagency p52, 187, 225, 275, 346, 405
Graeme Knox p53
Liv friis-larsen p53, 66, 319, 367
Leungchopan p54
Jason Vandehey p56, 221
Norman Chan p57, 359, 397
Irina Afonskaya p58, 155, 271, 390
Alexander Chaikin p64, 178
Andy Z. p68, 267, 209
Buruhtan p69
Ravshan Mirzaitov p69, 157, 233
Gabriela_L p73
Justin Black p73, 128, 217, 361
Makarova Viktoria p74, 322, 346, 381
Helen & Vlad Filatov p77, 165, 175
Petrenko Andriy p77, 380
EpicStockMedia p94, 263, 314, 345
Sandra Cunningham p95, 366, 379
Tim Roberts Photography p95, 368, 411
photofriday p98, 287, 317
Olga Lyubkina p99, 247, 349, 375
Patryk Kosmider p102
Mr. Green p103
Marie C Fields p104, 182
Silver-john p120, 230, 294
Maugli p121
blinow61 p121, 147, 256, 296, 356
gary718 p127, 148, 247
cptsai p127
Girish Menon p130
Konstantin Sutyagin p131
ANP p132, 169, 394
Vladimir Mucibabic p134

Rafal Cichawa p135
Nestor Noci p136
Simon Krzic p139
Ella_K p139
NizamD p141, 240
SoloHielo p142
Stacy Funderburke p143
Carlos Neto p146
Manuel Fernandes p147, 220, 403
Kirill Mikhirev p150, 166, 224, 315
Mike Bauer p151, 222
Paul D Smith p152
JetKat p155
Tramper p160, 213, 372
Gianna Stadelmyer p161, 212, 303, 398
Manamana p164, 404
Moonlightbg p168, 310, 381
Scirocco340 p169
@erics p174, 234, 378, 395
Nikolay Stefanov Dimitrov p179, 311, 375
Anna Diederich p179
Herbert Kratky p183, 357
Mariano Heluani p183, 269, 344
Pres Panayotov p184, 407, 408, 291, 304
Tamara Kulikova p186
Scirocco340 p187
Paul Tobeck p190, 271, 402, 316
goldsaint p191
Laurin Rinder p209
Vitaly Titov & Maria Sidelnikova p210, 340, 388, 391
rSnapshotPhotos p228
Simon Krzic p233
Dan Breckwoldt p236
Jorge Pedro Barradas de Casais p237, 253, 354, 369
PavelSvoboda p237, 282
MBphotography p238
Fototechnic p241
claudio zaccherini p241
hunta p257
chomplearn p263
Harald Toepfer p266
Buruhtan p270
Gate p275, 323
Julie Lubick p276
Radhouse, p295, 367, 378, 334
Bill Perry p297
Doug Lemke p299, 379
Sebastian Knight p300
nostal6ie p301

Marcio Jose Bastos Silva p305
Scirocco340 p318
Bertold Werkmann p320
Oleksiy Mark p321, 385
Brykaylo Yuriy p324
gary718 p328
Serg64 p345
Cptsai p348
Petrenko Andriy p348b, 393t, 411
Wallenrock p353
Jorge Pedro Barradas de Casais p354–355, 369, 386–387, 410
NizamD p359
IKO p360
Riaan van den Berg p373
Adrian Baras p373
Simon Krzic p376, 399
Kaido Karner p377
Pavel Mitrofanov p397
nostal6ie p400
Junker p401
Stacy Funderburke p401

All of the above are represented by Shutterstock.

Whilst every effort has been made to credit contributors, Quarto would like to apologise should there have been any omissions or errors, and would be pleased to make the appropriate correction for future editions of the book.